saying

Yes!

to you and your life

thriving

in recovery

the *Living in Alignment* approach

Darcy S. Clarke

Contents

APPENDICES

IN DEDICATION

This book is dedicated to all people whose lives are adversely affected or cut short by the pervasive impact of substance or process addictions. May they find healing in the promise that all their life circumstances are significant and intended to deepen their transformation.

Foreword

DARCY S. Clarke's *Saying* **Yes!** *to You and Your Life* places your sustained recovery from substance or process addictions in the context of your *spiritual journey:* discovering and *coming home to yourself.*

In Darcy's inclusive understanding of the *spiritual core* of your transformation process, simply *detoxing* under medical supervision is not going to change your life. Even after your body has returned to substance-free functioning, you will be in danger of *relapse* unless you face the *reality* of your addiction: the pervasive *lure* of your using patterns.

If you choose the option of recovery in a residential treatment setting, just making it through the program is not enough to change your life. You will predictably be in danger of *multiple relapses* if you do not use this opportunity to break away from your self-defeating 'baggage' and discover your own path of healing: fully embracing your present and past with its pain, disappointment, self-hate, and suffering.

Saying Yes! to you, your life, and the promise of your healing will open the door to discovering the hidden insights, gifts, and lessons of your life journey, starting today.

If you use this book to explore your spiritual core, you will discover the resources and power to pursue your own process of healing and transformation.

Wayne Marshall Jones, editor

Preface

YOU *cannot sustain your recovery without transformation. Your transformation begins with your recovery*. This book is intended to illuminate the perennial wisdom and significance of this perspective.

These two statements are intrinsically interconnected. You can't have one without the other, and both are essential to shift from merely surviving or just getting by to a *state of thriving* in your life.

From the perspective of Living in Alignment, *recovery* is more than getting and staying clean and sober. Many people are clean and sober, but are *'white-knuckling it.'* This term describes those who are not using, but who still exhibit characteristics of someone who is using: isolating, being secretive, preoccupied with remaining abstinent or focusing on not using, emotionally distant/unavailable, not in touch with your reality or shut down, anxious, unhappy, irritable, resentful, angry, lying/deceptive, depressed, having low self-esteem, insomnia, in denial, immature, insecure, etc.

To experience *thriving in recovery*, in addition to getting and staying clean and sober, it will be necessary to

❖ *identify* and work through *underlying causes* that keep your dependence in the driver's seat

❖ *reclaim* your *personal power* that you have given away to addictions, to other people, to other conditions (physical, mental, emotional), to events, and/or to limiting conditioning (beliefs, perceptions, expectations, behaviors, attitudes, and the like) about yourself, Source energy/ spirituality, addiction, other people, and life

❖ begin *Living in Alignment*, which requires developing a *conscious connection* with your soul (Source energy within) and listening to and following its guidance and prompting.

This book was written for people who have Substance Use Disorders (substance abuse/addiction) and/or behavioral addictions. The information presented here is intended to offer a broader perspective on the origin and treatment of *dependence*. Emphasis is placed on your recovery and the process involved in this life-transformative undertaking. It is my hope that this book will inspire and motivate you and generate an optimistic attitude toward *committing to your recovery* and moving forward in your life.

It is also for spouses/significant others, family members, and friends who are in relationships with people who have these conditions, as well as for people working in the recovery field. May your understanding of these conditions be illuminated and your interactions/treatment strategies be modified accordingly.

Note: Please refer to the Glossary (page 233) for definitions of terms used in this book.

1

Struggling to Stay Clean and Sober

ASSISTING people in their recovery process has been one of the most *challenging, heart breaking*, and at the same time *rewarding experiences* in my life, both personally and professionally. As I reflect on my work with people in recovery from substance and process/behavioral addictions, what echoes in my mind are the *voices of people's struggle to stay clean and sober*.

For some people, both getting and staying clean and sober are obstacles to their recovery. But for many others it's not getting clean and sober that's the issue; it's *staying clean and sober and living in recovery* that is daunting. Indeed, for people who have experienced *multiple relapses*, recovery from addictions is often seen as 'Mission Impossible' and/or something that they're not sure they want.

The *anguish* that many people experience about remaining clean and sober feels overwhelming, a distress that *exacerbates* existing mood, anxiety, or other co-occurring disorders (and in some cases may very well *cause* these conditions). When you add *the consequences* of people's using behavior and the subsequent impact on all aspects of their inner and outer reality, their *distress level* goes sky high. This distress often becomes unbearable, experienced as a sense of *hopelessness* and despair, and becoming a *trigger* to start using again.

Between a Rock and a Hard Place

Many people in *early recovery* think that they're caught between a rock and a hard place, that there's no way out, and that their substance abuse/addiction and co-occurring disorders have them immobilized in a headlock. They feel utterly defeated, helpless, and hopeless!

For some people this bleak state of affairs becomes the eye-opener for recognizing that they've become *powerless* and have no control over their dependence and/or that their co-occurring disorders need to be identified and dealt with. In turn, this recognition becomes the *impetus* to seek treatment/ recovery.

For others the recognition/acknowledgment of an addiction and/or a co-occurring disorder is perceived as a *personal failure*. If not directly and properly addressed, this perception can produce what is referred to as *toxic shame*. When this occurs a person views him-/herself as *defective* and his/her life as *a mistake*. Toxic shame can become mentally and emotionally overwhelming and incapacitating, leading to living in a *shame-based* reality.

W HETHER you believe
you can or can't,
you're right!
—Henry Ford

A person living in a shame-based reality

❖ has *low* self-esteem

❖ thinks that something is *seriously* wrong with him/her

❖ is bothered by his/her *shortcomings*

❖ thinks he/she is *permanently* flawed

❖ sees him-/herself as *failing* to reach his/her goals in life

❖ thinks he/she is a *bad* person

❖ believes that he/she is

◆ a *sinner* in the eyes of God (if religious)

◆ not as *smart* as his/her fellow workers

◆ not as *attractive*/kind/interesting as others

◆ not *good* enough

◆ not *lovable*

and other such self-deprecating descriptors.

People who have toxic shame experience a lot of anger, are full of rage, and often become *'victims'* who blame everyone else for their lot in life and are not willing to see their part or take any responsibility for what has happened to them.

They often hold to the perception that they're *innocent victims* of life's cruel tricks (or the antics of some menacing higher Power). Furthermore, anything that they consider to be *bad, wrong, or nega-*

tive in their lives should never have happened to them. They are often unaware of how their *limiting beliefs and ways of thinking* are getting in their way, perpetuating *'victim consciousness'*, and preventing them from receiving the treatment they require and moving forward in their lives.

With this lack of awareness, they find themselves *caught up in drama* (their own or others') and not able/willing to examine the particulars of how they are *co-creating* their realities. They are never getting better, only getting bitter!

Falling into the Pit

Many people in early recovery are *angry at the situation* they find themselves in and *angry at themselves* for becoming dependent. They are *incensed* at the thought that they have become addicted and that this could be happening to them. *'Why me?'* is a common rhetorical question.

It is common for people in early recovery to *fall into the cognitive pit* that their lives are in ruins, and for good reason, especially if everyone and everything has been taken or pushed away or destroyed as a consequence of their using behavior.

❖ How could this be happening to *me?*

❖ The *damage* I've done is unforgivable and beyond repair!

❖ I'm too far gone in my addictions; there is *no hope* for me!

❖ I'm a *lost cause*; there is no way back!

The reality of having addiction is often one of the most difficult admissions/truths people face in early recovery. For many the *recognition* that they have become powerless over and dependent upon substance and/or process addictions is unacceptable.

After all, for many people *their addictions had become their best friends and allies*. Their addictions are what pulled them through the worst of times: when they were down and out, feeling lost, confused, and/or overwhelmed. Their addictions also helped them celebrate the good times and/or seemingly prolonged the good times. Their addictions never judged, shamed, blamed, found fault, or sent them on a guilt trip. Their drugs of choice were loyal, true friends, always there in times of need (or so they thought in their delusion).

Cursing a Higher Power

As a result, it is more common than not for many in early recovery to *remain in denial* about the severity of the predicament in which they find themselves. Avoiding and/or minimizing are common.

Many experience themselves as victims of some nasty scheme to ruin their lives. Old wounds of *neglect, abandonment, and betrayal* surface, and they find themselves cursing a higher Power.

Here are some of the more common statements and questions that are heard repeatedly:

❖ If there *is* a higher Power, why wasn't this prevented?

❖ Why do *I* have addictions, and/or why do *I* have a mental or physical condition in the first place?

❖ What kind of higher Power would **allow** these bad/negative/horrible things to happen to me (or for that matter, to anyone)?

❖ Are the circumstances I'm facing **punishment** for my wrongdoings?

❖ I did everything the way I was supposed to, and **this** is what I get in return!

❖ Where is the **justice?**

❖ Damn right I'm **mad!** I was just minding my own business trying to manage my life and move forward as best I could!

❖ This is a kick below the belt. I'm angry, and I have a **right** to be angry!

It's common for many people to think along the lines that their addiction is some kind of sick game that this menacing, sadistic, cruel, unloving, and merciless old man up in the sky devised. **Misunderstandings, misinterpretations, and misgivings** have led many people to conclude that

❖ they want **nothing to do with** a higher Power

❖ there **is** no higher Power

❖ they are **all alone** in the universe

❖ there is **no meaning** and/or purpose to life

❖ life is fraught with **hardship** and **suffering,** and then you **die!**

They wake up to the realization that they have lost *so* much (for some it's everything: time, health, loved ones, careers, money) that they *don't want to go on living*.

On the other hand, some people with substance abuse and dependence issues *refuse* to acknowledge that they're hurting themselves or others.

Many people in early recovery are also *angry at a higher Power*. The abandonment and betrayal they feel towards a higher Power is deemed unforgivable. They feel that they did nothing wrong, so why did all these *'bad'* (hurtful, damaging, harmful, destructive, ruinous, unhealthy, injurious, detrimental) things happen to them? They're outraged! In their minds this experience called life is a worthless game of lies, deceit, injustices, suffering, and hardship they don't want any part of. A *common mindset* is that there's *no escaping* the world of addiction.

Giving Away Your Power

And so *the last thing* some people in recovery want to hear is that *addiction is an incurable disease,* and that *once an alcoholic/addict, always an alcoholic/addict.* To hear over and over again that they're *powerless* over addiction adds further pain and anguish, is infuriating, and/or for others is insulting to their intelligence.

This is especially the case for many *younger people* who are in the prime of their lives, who feel omnipotent, who are in the process of individuating and differentiating. ***They don't like to be told*** that they can't use anymore. With this population, ***alcohol and drugs*** are often seen as the conduit to good times: they believe they can't have one without the other. Using is so much a part of the culture that it's everywhere. They think they would have no social life if they stopped using. And besides, many of their peers are able to use and do not have substance abuse or dependence issues. So they're understandably angry at the situation they find themselves in. Facing this reality is very disturbing and often ***met with great resistance, antagonism, and aversion.***

For others, acknowledging that they have addiction is synonymous with ***declaring defeat*** and giving up their power. This is perceived and experienced as a huge letdown! The irony is that they have inadvertently and unknowingly (subconsciously) given up their power to dependence on substances and behaviors.

So they will

❖ ***deny or minimize***

❖ ***attempt to control*** their using behavior

❖ ***be furious*** about the situation and/or at themselves

❖ move into a position of trying to ***reason with their addiction***.

The ensuing struggle may go on for many years.

Many people—both those who abuse and those who are dependent—are able to perform their duties, be functional, and limit their using behaviors. The last thing they want to do is to acknowledge having an addiction, for in so doing they see this as an *indicator of weakness*.

Your Illusion of Control

People who want to feel powerful don't want to think or feel that they've given away their power. Especially if their *egoic mind* thinks that it can and should maintain power and control! They will persist in their *attempts to control their using behavior* and their lives to the best of their abilities. Many people are seemingly successful at doing this, and will continue doing so for many years until the *consequences* of their using behavior catch up with them.

This plays out in very destructive/harmful/ruinous ways in all of their relationships (including with themselves) and in all aspects of their lives, such as

❖ car accidents/*multiple* injuries

❖ physical complications/*conditions*

❖ mental and emotional *'dis-ease'*/conditions

❖ antagonism/alienation/*hostility* from family members/people they love

❖ separation/*divorce*/custody battles

❖ loss of employment/*career* opportunities

❖ loss of *friends*

❖ loss of *energy*/motivation/inspiration/zest for life

❖ loss of *interest* in social, recreational activities that were once important

❖ financial *ruin*

❖ disregard/*violation* of their values, morals, and code of ethics

❖ spiritual *dis*connection

From the get-go many experienced substance use as a *perfect* solution to whatever issue, problem, or challenge they were facing: it eased their physical/ emotional pain, stopped the self-judgment, shaming, fault-finding, and guilt-tripping messages in their mind, changed their mood, was energizing, released inhibitions, cast problems aside, etc. This felt very natural: a solution to take the edge off.

Substance use *alters* our brain chemistry and thus our functioning. At the onset people with substance abuse and dependence are often *naive* about the danger involved in their use of addictive drugs (illicit or prescribed). Little did they know at first that what their mind/body perceived as the answer/ solution that would *make them feel better and set them free* would turn out to be *their worst predicament and imprisonment.*

A large percentage of people who use mood-altering substances have a *chemical imbalance* in their brains. They are using their substance/drug of choice to *self-medicate* pre-existing mental/emo-tional/physical conditions.

Journal entry of a person with addiction: a snapshot of my using days

by an anonymous user

*As I think back on my using days, I was **under the impression** that I was coming to my own rescue. That I was focusing on a solution and had seemingly found one. I really thought that I was actually helping myself. My drugs of choice come across as being an answer (if not **the** answer) to my distress, issues, problems, challenges, concerns, troubles, hardship, suffering, setbacks, unhappiness, regrets, misfortune, heartache, and the like.*

*__I was looking outside__ myself for answers, not knowing that the answers were to be found inside. It is true that **addictive substances are effective** in altering brain chemistry. Early on I sometimes felt it almost instantly, but it was **only temporary and with damaging results and terrible side effects**. My drugs of choice soon became my best friend, or so I thought for a long time, longer than I'd like to admit. They altered my mood, changed the way I felt about something or many things, helped me not to think and/or feel and to suppress, deny, minimize, or otherwise avoid certain aspects of my reality.*

*My drug use **seemingly helped me to develop** selective hearing, thinking, seeing, and feeling. Wow! This was more than I imagined/bargained for, too good to be true, and yes, when all was said and done, it **was** too good to be true. Even after my using behavior resulted in serious damage to my* *body and other (if not all) areas of my life and the lives of others, and the consequences mounted, my solution was to disregard the voice within and continue using. All the while, **my tolerance was increasing**.*

*Although the '**fix**' had produced the immediate results I was looking for, little did I know (or didn't want to know) that it was developing a need for (dependence on) 'instant gratification.' The so-called '**quick fix**' solution turned out to be an imposter. It was not life-giving or life-sustaining. On the contrary, this 'instant gratification' was just temporary relief that **only masked** whatever I was attempting to escape from, hide from, numb out from, or otherwise avoid or suppress—making false promises of a life of bliss, superior to any other means.*

And it worked (or so I thought and/or wanted to believe) as long as I kept using my drug of choice.

*With each use, however, my relationship with my drug of choice was creating adverse side effects. Although present, the question—**To use or not to use?**—was drowned out by **the pleasurable sensations** pulsating throughout my mind/body. That sense of **relief** was beyond compare. With the passing of time, however, I continued to use not so much to get high anymore, but to just **feel normal** and/or to **avoid** the inevitable repercussions— because now I'd developed **dependence** evidenced by increased tolerance and withdrawal symptoms.*

*As the **consequences piled up** and started having a greater impact, I found my mind justifying, denying, minimizing, and rationalizing my drug use. Protecting my habit with **mental defenses** became a preoccupation, along with my using behavior. **Denial** became my most effective defense strategy. I became so adept at this that I was even able to convince/fool myself into believing my own lies.*

*I'm **angry at myself** and angry at the drugs I'm taking. The power and control I thought I had has been given over to my drugs of choice. They now have complete **control** of my mind, my body, and my life. My sense of having it together—of feeling like I'm **omnipotent** and in control—has been replaced with feelings of **powerlessness**, guilt, shame, fear, blame, and anger—at myself, at others, at life, at a higher Power, and with being dependent. All gets enmeshed/scrambled, and I'm finding it very difficult to keep it all in order. Who did what, when, to whom, where, and why: it all gets rolled into **one big entanglement** of more of what I didn't want and tried to escape from in the first place. Time, people, places, events turn into one big **blur**.*

*Differentiating between what really happened is confusing/overwhelming, and the truth? Well, that's hidden in the **lies** and **deceit** I laid on myself and others. Instead, a sense of helplessness and hope-lessness ensues. I have become a **hostage** in my own mind and body, and now there seems to be **no escape**.*

RECOVERING

As I walk down this road,
this new road I have taken,
I glance back over my shoulder,
perhaps I am mistaken.

Yet I see once again,
as I've doubted before
that those days are behind me
I'm not hers anymore.

Sometimes the images
creep into my head
of the smoke swirling and whirling
as I looked almost dead.

A shiver slips
and crawls up my spine
I again reassure myself
that this life is mine.

It surprises me to see
that I've done so well
I almost don't believe
I've escaped that living hell.

She had a grip on me
like nothing ever has before
She burrowed into my brain
so that I could think no more.

Now I am my own,
steering my own way
Turning to God, not her
to be sure not to stray.

I don't have to be weak,
I don't have to give in
She is powerless to me
No longer will she win.

2

Saying *Yes!* to You and Your Life

SAYING *Yes!* to you and to your life is about *becoming your own best friend and ally.* This cannot truly happen until *you begin liking and loving yourself.* People who have abuse and dependence issues are often unable or *have great difficulty opening their hearts* to themselves, let alone becoming their own best friend and ally.

Opening your heart to yourself and to your life is essential to begin the process of liking and in turn loving yourself. The *qualities* of an open heart (see page 87) are necessary to penetrate and take down the mental walls/defenses that your mind/intellect has erected. It is these walls/defenses that keep your heart closed and/or prevent it from opening to yourself and to living your life. Behind these mental defenses are unresolved issues, shame, guilt, anger, fear, and emotional pain.

From the Living in Alignment perspective, having *low self-esteem* (or an inferiority complex) is an indicator that your heart has been closed to yourself and to your life. The more you open your heart to yourself and to your life, the more you will begin liking and loving yourself. *Developing self-esteem is contingent upon your ability to like and love yourself and your life. This cannot happen until you open your heart.*

Judging, shaming, blaming, fault-finding, and *guilt-tripping* yourself are indicators that your heart is closed, and your cue to open your heart to yourself in that moment.

Identifying, challenging, and in turn modifying and/or replacing limiting beliefs about yourself and your life will be necessary to take down your mental defenses that are keeping your heart closed.

As your heart begins to open to yourself, you'll become receptive to getting to know yourself—instead of being at odds with your mind/intellect, your body, and your life.

An Act of Love

Genuine self-esteem is *an inside job.* It is self-generated and, once established, *needs nothing from the outside.* In other words, *people who have healthy self-esteem are able to esteem themselves from within.*

Getting off the fence and getting into recovery is one way of coming to your own rescue. It is *an act of love* for yourself. Without self-love, recovery from addictions will be a *futile* endeavor resulting in *failure.* Opening your heart to yourself and to your life is the key to unlocking the door to the most powerful of all the healing resources: the quality of love. Addiction is always *a poor substitute* for love.

YOU will have no power
to change your life
until you first recognize that you have a problem.

What keeps you from Saying *Yes!* to You and to Your Life?

Here is a list of common reasons that prevent people from ***opening their hearts*** to themselves and to their lives. Check ☑ the ones that apply to you.

- ☐ feeling unworthy/***undeserving*** of happiness, enjoyment, love, nurturance, and fulfillment
- ☐ being unable to hold myself accountable/take ***responsibility*** for my life
- ☐ being ***conflicted*** about many things that have happened to me
- ☐ ***despising*** myself and my life
- ☐ my ***fear*** of change
- ☐ feeling ***overwhelmed*** with my life
- ☐ thinking that it's not possible or that it is ***too late*** to begin my new life
- ☐ believing that living my life is ***too difficult***
- ☐ thinking or feeling my life is ***meaningless***
- ☐ my ***regrets***
- ☐ feeling I am ***defective***
- ☐ my ***low*** self-esteem
- ☐ being immobilized by ***shame***
- ☐ feeling ***guilty*** about my using behavior and/or about not living in integrity
- ☐ ***unresolved*** issues getting in my way

☐ *anger* at myself

☐ judging/*criticizing* myself

☐ thinking that I'm a bad/sinful/*evil* person

☐ *self-hate*/being uncomfortable in my own skin

☐ inability to *accept* mistakes I've made

☐ feeling that I and my life are a *mistake*

☐ other:

Not saying **Yes!** or being on board for yourself and your life plays itself out in

❖ *self-sabotage:* when your mind unconsciously destroys, damages, or obstructs relationships, careers, and living up to your full potential

❖ *self-deprivation:* living in a poverty mentality, not addressing and/or getting your needs/wants met, restricting/limiting pleasure, martyrdom

❖ *self-punishment:* being accident-prone, creating hardship or suffering, being a victim, caught up in drama—yours or others'

❖ living in a *shame-* and/or *fear-based reality*.

PAIN:
The effort required
to cling to old ideas and old behaviors.

3

Thriving in Your Recovery

FROM the Living in Alignment perspective, *thriving* in your recovery cannot happen until you first *let yourself off the hook* (so to speak) and *forgive yourself* for your abuse of or dependence upon substances and/or behaviors. Your using behavior was the result of being **unaware** of (or choosing to keep your head in the sand about) the **underlying causes** that kept your substance abuse/addiction in the driver's seat.

Your reasons for choosing to use in the first place seemed to make good sense at the time, although you later found out otherwise. Being angry and holding resentment toward yourself is counterproductive and will only interfere with and jeopardize your recovery.

The act of forgiving yourself for the poor choices and decisions you've made is another way in which you open your heart up to yourself and come to your own rescue. Instead of beating yourself up, look for the *lessons being offered* in your choices and decisions to use and continue using. In turn, allow these lessons to be *transformative* by increasing your awareness/understanding of the particulars involved and integrating this new knowledge into your thinking and behaviors.

Thriving in your recovery will include

❖ *reclaiming* or taking back your power from addictions and other conditions, other people, places, events, experiences, and limiting beliefs/ ways of thinking

❖ identifying and working through the underlying *causes* of your dependence

❖ identifying your human and soul *needs* and getting them met

❖ developing a *conscious* partnership with your soul

What keeps you on the fence regarding your recovery?

Identify and check ☑ *your* reasons for being *on the fence* or uncommitted to your recovery.

☐ I've given up on *myself*.

☐ I've given up on my *life* or on life in general.

☐ I've given up on a *higher Power*.

☐ There are too many *adverse* consequences to my using behavior.

☐ My emotional pain is *unbearable*.

☐ It's *too late* to turn my life around.

☐ I feel that I'm a failure and my life is *doomed*.

☐ I tried to quit many times and *failed* repeatedly.

☐ I feel *hopeless* about my situation.

- ☐ I'm angry at *Source energy*.
- ☐ I'm *afraid* to ask for help.
- ☐ I feel *abandoned* by Source energy.
- ☐ I think that receiving assistance equates to *weakness*.
- ☐ My using lifestyle/friends are the *only* life I know.
- ☐ I have no *direction* in my life.
- ☐ I'm not wanting/ready to take *responsibility* for my life.
- ☐ My drug of choice is my *best* friend.
- ☐ My life is too *harsh* and I can't cope with it.
- ☐ I'm a *loser*.
- ☐ I have *nothing* to live for.
- ☐ It's *too late* for me.
- ☐ Life is *meaningless*.
- ☐ I can't deal with/*manage* my life without using.
- ☐ Drugs keep my depression, anxiety, or other mental/emotional conditions *in check*.
- ☐ Drugs give me energy/*stamina*.
- ☐ Drugs make me feel *powerful*.
- ☐ Drugs help me to overcome my *inhibitions*.
- ☐ I don't want to *feel* my emotional pain.
- ☐ I think I can *control* my using behavior.

☐ I don't want to be digging up my *past.*

☐ I don't like the idea that there is more *wrong* with me than having addiction.

☐ I have too much *pressure* to succeed.

☐ My *unhappiness.*

☐ My *heartache.*

☐ My *despair.*

☐ My *setbacks.*

☐ Holding onto my *secrets.*

☐ My *regrets.*

☐ My hardship, troubles, *misfortune.*

What does your using behavior offer you that you don't experience when you're clean and/or sober? Answering this question will illuminate the causes underlying your using behavior.

Living in Alignment will assist you to live up to your full potential by *preventing your mind/intellect from interfering* in your daily life.

This is accomplished by teaching your human self/mind that its rightful function is to be in service of your soul. Instead of allowing your intellect to *override* your intuition, you can learn to *defer* to your soul for guidance and directives. In turn, you can utilize your mind's skill base to follow through in taking care of the details.

The more *externally resourced* you are, the more your egoic mind is unable or unwilling to give up control—or more accurately, *the illusion of control*. Living in Alignment also emphasizes the importance and *necessity* of meeting the needs of *both* your human self and your soul. This is about *embodying both your humanity and your spirituality* and becoming receptive to the experiences you are *intended* to have in this lifetime.

RISK

To laugh is to risk appearing the fool
To weep is to risk appearing sentimental

To reach out to others is to risk involvement
To expose feelings is to risk exposing your true self

To place your ideas, your dreams before a crowd
    is to risk their loss
To love is to risk not being loved in return

To live is to risk dying
To hope is to risk despair
To try is to risk failure

But risks must be taken,
because the greatest hazard in life is to do nothing.

The person who risks nothing,
does nothing, has nothing, and is nothing.

You may avoid suffering and sorrow,
but you cannot learn, feel, change, grow, love, live.

Chained by your attitudes, you are a slave,
you forfeited your freedom.

Only the person who risks can be free.

IT'S the Journey that's Important...
Life, sometimes so wearying
Is worth its weight in gold
The experience of traveling
Lends a wisdom that is old

    Beyond our 'living memory'
    A softly spoken prayer:
    "It's the journey that's important,
    Not the getting there!"

Ins and outs and ups and downs
Life's road meanders aimlessly?
Or so it seems, but somehow
Leads us where we need to be,

    And being simply human
    We often question and compare....
    "Is the journey so important
    Or the getting there?"

And thus it's always been
That question pondered down the ages
By simple men with simple ways
To wise and ancient sages ....

    How sweet then, quietly knowing
    Reaching destination fair:
    "It's the journey that's important,
    Not the getting there."

        —John McLeod

4

Experiencing Transformation

WHAT if it is true that you are *intended* to have transformative experiences throughout your lifetime?

Transformation is a lifelong process of *integrating insights, gifts, and lessons* from your life experiences. Transformation sustains an *internal shift* in your awareness: focusing on the *life calling* you are intended to have and enabling you to accomplish it in the context of your life circumstances while also meeting your human needs.

Transformation is about change. And when you stop to think about it, *change is a constant*—a given in your life!

All of life is undergoing change; change is consciousness (energy) in motion. *By resisting the changes* that are occurring in your life, you're attempting to interfere with Source energy and thus with the *flow* of your life. This will *always* cause needless hardship and suffering.

The six phases of *the death and rebirth cycle* are

❖ *conception* (creation, genesis, beginning)

❖ *gestation* (formation, development, incubation)

❖ *birth* (emerging, bringing forth, producing)

- ❖ *growth* (blossoming, flourishing, thriving)
- ❖ *maturation* (ripening, coming to fruition)
- ❖ *death/transformation* (completion of a cycle, lesson, goal, relationship, career, idea, chapter in your life, developmental stage, etc.)

The death and rebirth cycle is *a natural process* playing out and repeated in nature and in all aspects of your life throughout your lifetime, as depicted in the seasons of the year, in the cycles of the moon, in the stages of your physical growth/development, and in your relationships, goals, ideas, careers, etc.

Transforming Your Past/Present

The Living in Alignment approach *reframes your recovery process as an opportunity to transform your past and/or your present situation*. In part this is about experiencing a metaphoric death and rebirth by identifying and in turn letting go of aspects of your life (past or present) that you have outgrown, that are getting in your way, or that prevent you from moving on with your life and living up to your greatest potential.

Although *developing a healthy ego is necessary and important* in and of itself, it is inadequate and incapable of creating fulfillment in your life if you do not also create a conscious relationship with your core or essential self—your soul.

Experiencing *sustainable transformation* is about having a true *spiritual awakening*. It is your *birthright*, an experience available to everyone.

It is necessary to *transcend your 'waking' state* in order for this to happen. You can begin by being receptive to the concept that *multiple levels* of consciousness exist. More specifically, that *the unseen world is as real as the world before your eyes.* This is not about denying the value or worth of your 'waking' state, or downplaying the significance of experiencing it fully. It's about acknowledging the reality of the unseen world and your vital *connection* to it.

When you shift your consciousness from your 'waking' state to your *awakened* state, you can live in the world with *greater creativity and energy* at your disposal.

Finding Your Bliss

You may have an intuitive sense that life is to be lived to the fullest. This is where the concept of *bliss* originates.

In your impatience, however, you may miss the insight that *you can truly come to know yourself only by fully engaging in life.* The more present and accounted for you are in dealing with everything that is going on within your life, the more you'll become *aware* of your dilemmas, challenges, fears, issues, and behaviors, along with your aptitudes, talents, skills, assets, strong points, shortcomings, faults, limitations, and deficiencies, etc. *Facing yourself and your life* is another way you open your heart to yourself and come to your rescue. *Being present* with yourself, with others, and with the experiences you're having offers you important information that is intended to facilitate and accelerate your personal growth and transformation.

Your lack of self-understanding and your inability to access your true desires suppress your urge toward spiritual bliss and divert your focus to the search for external security, pleasure, and power.

The more you go within to *listen to and follow the guidance and prompting of your soul*, the more you will experience the awakened state of *bliss*. This practice will help you function on a higher energy level (a natural high). This translates to becoming self-empowered: being with and staying in your power.

All of nature—trees, mountains, flowers, animals, insects, rocks—is *in bliss*. Living in Alignment facilitates creating *balance and harmony* in your life, which fosters experiencing *states of bliss* with increasing regularity.

Your experience of *bliss* is generated from the *quality of connection* you have with both your *humanity* and your *spirituality*, manifesting as energy, empowerment, happiness, desire, purpose, enjoyment, abundance, hope, fulfillment, and deep abiding love.

Experiencing Deeper Intimacy

When you leave behind your self-image of *trying to be someone other than your authentic self* and learn to *take your egoic mind out of the driver's seat*, you will no longer *struggle* with recovery.

When you're Living in Alignment with your soul, *you will recover* and gain complete trust and assurance that *your real power* (your self-empowerment) is derived from the *quality* of your *connection* with Source energy, not from status, material wealth, control/manipulation of others, or other external sources of the *illusion* of power. You will find that your *real* power is intended to serve as a means for experiencing *deeper intimacy* in all of your relationships (including your relationship with your human self *and* your soul) and in all aspects of your life: as a human being, as an energy/spiritual being, and as a planetary citizen.

Becoming empowered is an inside job. Your self-empowerment will lead to more enjoyment, passion, pleasure, spontaneity, and satisfaction in your life.

When you are self-empowered you do not require or strive for outside recognition or need to get caught up in impression management. None of this is necessary, for your self-esteem is derived from the *partnership* between your human self and your soul. The deeper and more loving your *soul connection* is, the more self-empowered you are.

Having ***direct experiences*** of the workings of Source energy will assist your mind/intellect to remove your defenses, become receptive to its wisdom, and defer to Source energy for guidance and directives.

Your freedom to be all that you are is contingent upon having ***a conscious relationship with Source energy***. This is a state of being that you'll be able to experience subjectively.

Discovering Your Spiritual Power

Could it be that your substance abuse or addiction is ***intended*** to be the impetus for you to understand that ***if you don't claim your real power, someone or something else*** (such as addiction) ***will?***

One of the universal principles of energy is that it cannot be created or destroyed; it can only be transformed. As ***your awareness increases*** in your recovery process, you will realize that your ***dependence*** on substances/processes is ***how you give away your real power*** (energy) as well as how you've coped with your underlying issues.

You *'mess up'* (relapse) when you are unable or unwilling to access and ***use your power*** to identify and resolve whatever issue, challenge, concern, or problem led to your using and dependence.

It is ***your responsibility*** to manage your energy as an energy being. The first step is to go inward and listen to hear the voice of your soul. This will be difficult without both openness and intent to do so.

You will come to recognize and acknowledge that *you have free will* in the choices you make, and that your decisions today have a direct *impact* on creating your reality.

Although you cannot erase the *consequences* of your using behavior, you *can* transform them. This is accomplished by opening your mind and heart to interpreting how *all circumstances of the past and/ or the present* are benefiting you.

Being in the Flow

Another universal principle is that energy is not static, but in a constant state of *evolution*—that the nature of all forms of life is to be changing.

Being in the flow of your life (being present and accounted for) gives you the opportunity to come alive, to experience *all* of who you are, and to be your authentic self! There you will truly recognize the significance of your life and find meaning and purpose. Being in the flow of your life is where opportunities and possibilities abound. You can discover and *live in this flow* by listening to and following the guidance and prompting from your soul.

Change is happening in all aspects of your life, whether or not you are *aware* of it, whether or not you *believe* this is true, and whether you *like* it or not!

Everyone and everything is constantly changing. It is the nature of Source energy, the creative force of the universe, to be constantly evolving. *Change* is one of the principles that govern how Source energy works in our universe.

In the context of your recovery, *you'll have no power to change your life until you first recognize that you have dependence*.

Remember that your recovery is intended to be *a transformative process*. Transformation of your dependence must come *from within*. By recognizing and acknowledging that *you're out of control*, you can reach out to and receive help from Source energy that's greater than anything you can access with your own effort and intellectual resources.

Your recovery will be *a lifelong journey* of becoming increasingly *aware:* of the *significance* of your presence, the *roles* you take on, your *spiritual* nature, *why* you're here, and the *insights, gifts, and lessons* being offered through the *trials and tribulations* of living in *your* physical body as you *interact* with human beings and other life forms on this journey called life.

Integrative Activity

On a blank sheet of paper, write: 'When I think of *Transformation* what comes to mind is…' For the next 7 minutes, write down nonstop whatever comes to mind as you repeat the word *Transformation*. It may be single words or statements. Do not edit. It's okay to repeat. Don't try to make sense or correlations. Then look at what you wrote. What jumps out? What catches your eye/captures your attention?

5

Living in Your Truth and Power

FROM the Living in Alignment perspective substance abuse, substance and behavioral addictions, and relapse are viewed as *wake-up calls*.

These conditions are indicators that you are *off track or heading in that direction*, meaning that you are *not* Living in Alignment. This happens when your human self/mind is not listening to and following the guidance and prompting from your core self—your soul (Source energy within). In this context, *abuse, addiction, and dependence* are a consequence of *spiritual deprivation*, and *a spiritual void* lies at the core.

When you're *not* Living in Alignment, your *egoic mind/intellect* is getting in your way. This translates to *deficient* functioning, because you're out of touch with your own *truth*—with what is real and alive for you! *Living in your truth* is synonymous with *being in your power*!

Self-empowerment is generated from being in a *conscious partnership* with Source energy. When you're Living in Alignment you are being internally resourced: listening to and following the guidance from your soul (Source energy within). Being in relationship with your soul is how you access *your deepest truth*: the meaning and purpose of your life, and *who you truly are*.

Your soul is the deepest, *most intimate aspect* of who you are. If you prefer, it is the universal consciousness (or higher Power) that dwells within you and all life forms.

Living in partnership with your soul will ensure that you become aware of and attend to *both* your human and soul needs as you come into and remain *in your power* and thus in the flow of your life.

As this occurs you will have increasing assurance that *everything* happening in your life is of *significance* and is intended to provide you with *maximum benefit*.

When you're *not living* in your own flow, you're *not* tuning into and attending to the needs of both your human self and your soul. You're *not* doing what you've been called to do; *not* allowing yourself to have the experiences you're intended to have; and *not living* up to your full potential.

Not living in the flow of your life will consume increasing amounts of your mental, emotional, and physical energy—with diminishing returns.

The purpose of wake-up calls is *to get the attention* of your human self/mind to *come back home* to and connect with your soul (Source energy within).

From the perspective of Living in Alignment, substance abuse/addiction/relapse are indicators that you're *not living* in your power. Knowing the particulars of when, why, and to whom you have *given away* your power is an important task in your recovery process.

It is equally important to know that *it is your responsibility to reclaim your power* from addiction and other conditions, other people, events, limiting beliefs/thinking, and behaviors. Keep in the forefront that when you don't claim your power, something (such as addictions) or someone else will.

Learn to identify your *wake-up calls*. They are your clues that you're either *off track* or headed in that direction. They are *warnings* that something is wrong: that you need to be taking *a closer look* at what's up for you that requires your attention.

Signs of Having Given Away Your Power

Here is a list of common indicators of having turned your power over to your mental, emotional, or physical conditions (addictions), to other people, or to limiting beliefs or thinking, events, unresolved issues, etc. Check ☑ the boxes that apply to you.

☐ internal or external *boundary* failures

☐ bodily tensions, aches, *pains*

☐ insomnia/*sleeping* disorders

☐ susceptibility to *stressors*

☐ *attention* deficits

☐ *impaired* thinking

☐ immune system complications/*disorders*

☐ *low* self-esteem/inferiority complex

☐ the creation and/or *exacerbation* of mental/emotional/physical conditions

☐ feeling like a punching bag/*disrespected*

☐ feeling impotent/helpless/hopeless/*despair*

☐ feeling *distressed*

☐ feeling that you've been taken *advantage* of

☐ feeling that you're being treated like a *doormat*

☐ feeling *violated*

☐ feeling powerless/weak/*diminished*

☐ feeling taken advantage of/*used*

☐ being *contemptuous*

☐ being vengeful and/or *vindictive*

How Do You Feel Emotionally When You've Given Away Your Power?

When you've given away your power, you will likely have a combination of feelings that vary and are impacted by the particulars of giving your power away (when, how, for how long, and to whom).

Check ☑ the emotions that apply to you:

☐ I feel resentful (toward myself and others)

☐ ...angry (at myself and others)

☐ ...ashamed

☐ ...guilty

☐ ...fearful/anxiety-ridden

☐ ...helpless

☐ ...hopeless

☐ ...distressed

☐ ...disappointed

☐ ...emotional pain

☐ ...depressed

☐ ...contemptuous

☐ ...despairing

☐ ...other:

Deepening in Your Recovery

In order to get your mind/intellect out of the way, you'll need to learn how to *stop trying to control* yourself, your life, and everyone and everything in it. What your mind thinks you need or want is often *at odds* with what your soul needs or what is actually in your own best interests. When this is the case your mind will be *in conflict* with your soul.

The more *externally resourced* you are (relying only on your mind), the more difficult it is for your human self to *hear* the guidance from your soul, and if it does, the more it will tend to *disregard* these directives. Likewise, the more accustomed you are to getting what you want when you want it, the more your mind will *cancel out* the voice of your soul if you don't *like* the guidance/prompting that is being offered.

A sure way of causing and/or perpetuating need-less hardship and suffering is ***not tuning in*** to deter-mine whether what your mind/intellect needs and wants is ***congruent*** with accomplishing your soul mission or calling in life (your best interests), which facilitates living up to your full potential.

Your egoic mind is the aspect of your mind that ***thinks it is in control*** and has to maintain control! Living in Alignment requires a ***change in your ori-entation:*** instead of primarily trusting your mind to be in the driver's seat, you learn to ***defer*** to your soul by listening to and following its guidance and prompting.

If you're seeking to experience the ***balance and harmony*** of a carefree, untroubled, easygoing life-style, where you're not consumed with concern or worry, or preoccupied with survival or the mundane aspects of life, you will need to ***develop the capacity to Trust and Surrender*** to your soul (Source energy within).

I am aware that this concept of trusting in and surrendering to Source energy may be foreign to you or sound like New Age mumbo-jumbo. It doesn't make sense to the logical, rational, linear side of your brain (the ego-aspect of your mind that thinks it has to control your life), and thus is easy for your mind to discard as rubbish.

I'm the first one to say it: ***don't believe anything*** you're reading here, but please ***don't discard it*** either until you have a *direct experience* of what I'm talking about.

This concept is intended to be *tested out subjectively:* you are the scientist and your life is the lab.

Having *direct experiences* of these concepts will prove their validity, practicality, effectiveness, and reliability to your mind.

Living in Alignment fosters a change in your perspective: a *merging* of your human self/mind with your soul to form *a loving partnership*. Developing a conscious union with your soul will be life-changing and prove to be the most life-giving and most life-sustaining decision you will ever make.

What Gets in the Way of Your Recovery?

It is *your mental processing*, largely influenced by societal conditioning, that gets in the way of your recovery, personal growth, and transformation. Your conditioning includes limiting beliefs, perceptions, attitudes, expectations, and behaviors.

Your life is intended to be an ongoing series of transformative experiences! All of your life circumstances—including your roles, situations, events, experiences, concerns, problems, challenges, conditions, personal issues, and the like—are offering you insights, gifts, and lessons. These offer you *important information* about what is happening in your life (both internally and externally), in the lives of others, and in the world around you. This information is intended to increase your awareness. You can learn to tune into the significance and the specifics of what is being offered in your interactions *while they're happening*.

You may have already noticed that whenever you *intend* to become increasingly aware and conscious, you are more present in your daily experiences.

When you *recognize* and *acknowledge* your insights, gifts, and lessons, they become the stimulus/springboard for your transformative experiences, while your *integration* of these ensures that your transformation is *sustainable* (long-lasting). Integrating your insights, gifts, and lessons into your thinking and behaviors increases your understanding, facilitating internal shifts that expand your mind and open your heart.

Living in Alignment is a *lifelong process and practice* of merging your humanity with your spirituality. This merging fosters authentic living. Every step in this deepening process will provide you with maximum benefit. The stronger your bond with your soul, the more you will experience living authentically.

This *merging* of your human self with your soul has a synergistic effect on both your human self/intellect and your soul, facilitating an increased sense of *freedom* in both your human self and your soul.

You will come to experience that this merging becomes the most powerful and rewarding of unions: a *partnership* that will ensure you remain self-empowered by *deepening* in your relationship with Source energy.

Reclaiming Your Power

The Living in Alignment process will reveal *to whom or what* you have given away your power and how to reclaim it in ways that are beneficial/ advantageous.

You will start *feeling more self-empowered* as soon as you begin reclaiming your power from your addictive behaviors, other people (parents, siblings, ex-spouses, misguided leaders, strangers), events, places, limiting beliefs and thinking patterns, actions, choices, and decisions.

Reclaiming your power is *not* about 'an-eye-for-an-eye', or who's right and who's wrong, or having to have the last word, or being vindictive. When your human self/intellect chooses to merge with your soul (Source energy within), your focus is no longer dictated by your egoic mind, or by needing to be vengeful, or make others wrong, or stay in 'victim consciousness'. Your focus is on gaining an understanding of the *significance* of the presenting circumstances, and in turn *integrating* your insights, gifts, and lessons (knowledge) into new ways of thinking and behaving.

Reclaiming your power is about bringing *a win/ win* perspective to *solving conflicts*, creating *unity consciousness* within your mind/intellect, and helping to facilitate it in all of your interactions.

Integrative Activity

For the next 7 minutes, write nonstop: 'When I think about **_reclaiming my power_**—from addictions, people, events, limiting beliefs/thinking, self-defeating behaviors, situations, various conditions, unresolved issues—what comes to mind is...' Review and reflect on what you wrote. What insights, gifts, and lessons did you receive?

DON'T Worry
Please don't worry
There's little effect

    I'm some kind of crazy
    A vague subject

The voices expressing
And very direct

    A daily reminder
    Nothing is perfect

No need to judge
I just _may_ be crazy

    Please don't worry
    Been looking up lately

The same in the morning
Just as with night

    Stop trying to save me
    I'll be all right

Forget your theories
I'm happy with me

    So please don't worry
    I'm finally free

    —Jeff West

6

Addiction: the Prevalent View

THE Living in Alignment approach to recovery is inclusive of the prevalent view of addiction as a *disease*. The Diagnostic and Statistical Manual of Mental Disorders, the American Society of Addiction Medicine, the American Medical Association, and other leading voices in the recovery field view Substance Use Disorder/Addiction as *a chronic disease of brain reward, motivation, memory, and related circuitry*.

Dysfunction in these circuits leads to characteristic biological, chemical, neurological, medical, psychological, emotional, social, political, economic, and spiritual manifestations/underpinnings. This is reflected in an individual's *pathological* pursuit of reward and/or relief by substance use and other behaviors despite harmful consequences.

The disease model defines addiction as being characterized by an inability to abstain consistently, impairment in behavioral control, craving, diminished recognition of significant problems with one's behaviors and interpersonal relationships, and a dysfunctional emotional response. Like other chronic diseases, addiction often involves cycles of *relapse* and remission. Without treatment or engagement in recovery activities, addiction is progressive and can result in disability or premature death.

The most important finding of research into a genetic role for alcoholism is that there is no such thing as a gene for alcoholism, nor can you directly inherit alcoholism.
—Lance M. Dodes MD

The cell's operations are primarily molded by its interaction with the environment, not by its genetic code.
—Bruce Lipton PhD

The 12-Step Programs and Beyond

For those in recovery, the Living in Alignment approach can serve to *augment, complement, or* (for others) *replace* 12-step programs. The Living in Alignment perspective acknowledges that working the 12 steps and receiving the support and fellowship that 12-step programs offer have been invaluable for millions of people since their inception. Indeed, 12-step programs have saved countless lives.

Many people view 12-step programs as *an important* (if not a necessary) *step* in their recovery process. The 12-step programs have been, and continue to be, successful in serving as a springboard, assisting people to reconnect with their childhood religion and/or develop new religious affiliations.

This is all fine if you believe in a monotheistic/authoritarian type of higher Power. But if for various reasons you don't believe in such an entity/deity, then you're left scratching your head and/or put off by the program's faith-based rhetoric.

Some people who are clean and sober as a result of having worked 12-step programs also feel that these programs are *lacking* as well.

A growing number of people have severed their religious affiliations and are exploring their spirituality outside the confines of organized religion. This is one reason why many people in recovery are leery of, outspoken about, or steer away from faith-based recovery programs and are ambivalent, skeptical, or otherwise resistant to 12-step programs.

For others 12-step programs have facilitated *a spiritual emergence/awakening*. Working through an unresolved issue (personal, familial, or spiritual) can often assist people to open up to working the 12 steps and/or utilizing the support and fellowship that is available through this organization.

Other people who find the 12-step programs helpful also want to *augment* what they are gaining from the 12-step programs by *exploring other paths to spirituality*, including practices such as shamanic work, meditation, sweat lodges, yoga, visualization, prayer, fasting, dance, martial arts, vision questing, chanting, singing, and exploring nature.

The Living in Alignment approach is *intended to enhance* 12-step programs. In fact, the Living in Alignment approach helps people *embody* 12-step principles in their daily lives. To gain the most benefit from the Living in Alignment approach, people need to be *clean and sober* in their recovery.

The Living in Alignment approach acknowledges that we are both human beings and spiritual beings. It might be easier for your mind to grasp the concept that *we are both human beings and energy beings*.

This proposition may seem **ludicrous** to someone who defers to the left hemisphere of his/her brain that is rational, linear, and logical. It may also come across as **paradoxical**, for it can sound strange or impossible that we can be living in physical bodies and at the same time be composed of energy.

If you are primarily externally resourced (believing that your physical body and the three-dimensional world or what you see with your eyes is all there is), this proposition may sound too far 'out there', 'woo-woo', or idiotic. It may be annoying and perceived as an **insult** to your intelligence. This is completely understandable if you have a reductionist, mechanistic, materialistic viewpoint.

It is also true, however, that **quantum physicists have verified** that you are composed of energy at the most fundamental level of your being. From this perspective, all matter (including your physical body) and everything you see with your eyes is energy that has been 'slowed down' enough to be visible and tangible. Since the beginning of time mystics and wise people have known and passed down the insight that (Source) energy is Consciousness itself—the **Ground** of your being.

SCARED and sacred are spelled with the same letters.
Awful proceeds from the same root word as awesome.
Terrify and terrific.
Every negative experience holds the seed
of transformation.
—Alan Cohen

7

Substance Abuse/Addiction: an Emerging View

THE Living in Alignment Model advocates the emerging view that substance abuse and addiction are *symptoms of underlying causes*. In other words addictions are *not* the problem; they are what people are *using* to cope with problems/underlying conditions.

Once the underlying causes are identified and sufficiently addressed, *your desires, urges, and/or cravings to use will be greatly diminished* or be absent altogether. In this healing process you will learn skills to manage all aspects of your reality (mental, emotional, physical, spiritual, behaviors). If and when 'triggers' to use are present, you can easily recognize them and deal effectively with them so that they no longer result in a relapse or pose a threat to your recovery.

To reiterate, your *substance abuse and addiction are not the problems*. The culprit is the reason or reasons *why* you started to use and *why* you continue to relapse once you've gone through detox. All *causes* of dependence are *within you*, and all *solutions* to remaining free from addictive substances are also *within you*.

The underlying causes of your dependence fall into four categories:

❖ your chemical imbalances

❖ your unresolved issues from the past or present

❖ your limiting beliefs and ways of thinking

❖ your maladaptive coping skills to manage life on its terms

Your Chemical Imbalances

Some of the indicators of having a chemical imbalance are: feeling terrible, not having enough energy or inability to slow down, physical illness, being nervous/anxious, being agitated, paranoid thinking, or being mentally in a fog.

Chemical imbalances can come from a variety of sources. They can be *biologically* and/or *medically based*, and this is something you will want to determine early on. *Reduced numbers of neurotransmitters can be both a consequence of chronic drug use and a risk factor for addiction.*

Unresolved events from the past or present will cause *distress* in your present life, creating a chemical imbalance.

Limiting or faulty beliefs you hold about yourself, a higher Power, addiction and other conditions, other people, and living your life, will cause you to behave in ways that are not advantageous, leading to *disappointment, frustration,* and *distress* that create chemical imbalance.

Your *inability to cope* with or effectively manage current circumstances in your life produces anxiety, frustration, stress, and fear, all of which create *'disease'* and lead to chemical imbalance.

The *foods* you eat, the *liquids* you drink, the *thoughts* you think, and the *emotions* you feel produce body secretions that release chemicals that go to your brain and create *feelings* such as anxiety, stress, depression, anger, joy, ecstasy, euphoria, and well being.

The *people* you associate with, the *organizations* you affiliate with, the *interests* and *activities* you engage in—all have an *impact* on your brain chemistry.

The more you live in *balance and harmony*, the more enjoyment, passion, satisfaction, connection, fulfillment, and contentment you will experience. You find balance and harmony in your life when your human intellect is Living in Alignment with your soul (Source energy within). This translates to developing a *conscious partnership* with your soul.

Your Unresolved Issues from the Past or Present

Your *unresolved issues* may be related to trauma or abuse (physical, sexual, intellectual, emotional, spiritual). Trauma is defined as any experience that is less than nurturing. Unresolved issues include personal and/or interpersonal conflicts that have not been identified or given sufficient attention, sorted out, or worked through, manifesting as

- guilt
- shame
- anger/resentment
- fear/anxiety
- emotional/physical pain
- worry
- confusion
- doubt

Unresolved issues from the past or present will consume excessive amounts of your time, attention, and energy. *Early trauma* (anything less than nurturing experiences) can result in impaired functioning of your prefrontal cortex (the part of your brain that is responsible for regulating complex cognitive, emotional, and behavioral functioning). For some people with addictive behaviors, this plays out as *valuing false wants* above real needs.

These unresolved issues can become detrimental, hindering, and overwhelming, often resulting in various mental, emotional, and physical conditions such as

- 'victim consciousness'
- self-sabotage
- fatigue/low energy
- mood disorders
- anxiety disorders

❖ chronic physical and/or emotional pain

❖ resentments

❖ shame- and/or fear-based realities

❖ obsessive/compulsive disorders

Your Limiting Beliefs and Thinking

Your beliefs and thought patterns are co-creating your reality on a moment-by-moment basis. Beliefs are what your mind deems to be true, and thus they have a direct influence impacting all aspects of your life. Identifying and examining your beliefs will prove to be one of your most valuable skills, for it will illuminate how your conditioning is *benefiting you* or *getting in your way.* Living in Alignment focuses on beliefs that are relevant to your recovery process, including your beliefs about *yourself, addiction, living your life, other people,* and *Source energy.*

Your *thought patterns* are the many ways you process information, including your comprehension, expectations, perceptions, assessments, judgments, attitudes, reasoning, evaluations, intentions, and insights.

Your limiting beliefs and ways of thinking

❖ *get in your way* of forming and experiencing nurturing and satisfying relationships with yourself, others, and living your life

❖ *prevent* you from living up to your full potential

❖ *prohibit* you from seeing the significance of your presence and the roles you take on

❖ *block* your mind from tuning into the meaning and purpose of your life

❖ *inhibit* your experience of vitality, abundance, enjoyment, happiness, passion, and fulfillment

❖ *restrain* you from manifesting your true desires/ dreams

❖ *stop* you from experiencing balance and harmony and regulating your energy

❖ *sabotage* your best intentions and aspirations

❖ *hinder* you from achieving your goals.

When you learn to *partner* with Source energy in accord with the principles that govern how our universe works, you will manifest wisdom, wholeness, awareness, spontaneity, empowerment, abundance, balance, harmony, passion, serenity, and fulfillment.

Your Maladaptive Coping Skills

This category is like the other three: although separate, they overlap and impact one another. Living in Alignment will help you identify and examine the *five primary symptoms of codependence* and how they are affecting, influencing, or playing out in your life, including

❖ difficulty esteeming yourself from within

❖ difficulty establishing and maintaining functional boundaries

❖ difficulty owning all aspects of your reality: mental, emotional, physical, spiritual, behaviors

❖ difficulty identifying and meeting your needs

❖ difficulty finding balance and living in harmony

The *essential life skills* involved in *healing the wounds of codependence* include

❖ learning to love yourself

❖ learning to protect yourself

❖ learning to own your reality

❖ learning to nurture yourself

❖ learning to live in moderation (in balance and harmony)

Living in Alignment will help you *identify* essential life skills you are lacking and offers a working understanding and skill base. You will learn five key life skills that prepare you to deal successfully with stressors, develop nurturing and satisfying relationships, live your life on its terms, and reach your full potential.

TO bring about the new
takes not just a development of the old,
but a radical leap forward –
revolutionary and transforming –
and that requires extra factors
that were not present before.

—Mark H. Prichard

MY Comfort Zone

I used to have a comfort zone
    where I knew I wouldn't fail.
The same four walls and busywork
    were really more like jail.

I longed so much to do the things
    I'd never done before,
But stayed inside my comfort zone
    and paced the same old floor.

I said it didn't matter that
    I wasn't doing much.
I said I didn't care for things
    like commission checks and such.

I claimed to be so busy with
    the things inside the zone,
But deep inside I longed for something
    special of my own.

I couldn't let my life go by
    just watching others win.
I held my breath; I stepped outside
    and let the change begin.

I took a step and with new strength
    I'd never felt before,
I kissed my comfort zone goodbye
    and closed and locked the door.

If you're in a comfort zone,
    afraid to venture out,
Remember that all winners were
    at one time filled with doubt.

A step or two and words of praise
    can make your dreams come true.
Reach for your future with a smile;
    success is there for you!

8

Sustaining Your Recovery

THE *distinguishing feature* of the Living in Alignment approach to sustainable recovery is the emphasis placed on assisting you to *get your mind* (your human self) *to work in partnership with your soul* (your spiritual self). Special attention is provided to those transitioning from religious orthodoxy to spirituality.

Your soul will work with your mind/human self to develop a *spiritual practice* that will deepen your connection with your soul (Source energy within) and with Source energy in other people and in nature. You will want to choose practices and modalities that inspire, that feel nurturing, that help quiet the chatter in your mind, relax your body, and open your heart, that take down your mental defenses and open your mind, that have a unifying quality, that remind you of your interconnectedness and interdependence with all life forms, and that draw out and help you express and share your gifts and talents with the world.

The Living in Alignment approach to recovery *fosters, facilitates, and helps to ensure that you experience sustainable transformation*. This is accomplished by reclaiming your power from substance and process addictions, from people, from events, from limiting beliefs and thinking, from unresolved issues in your current experiences or in the past, and by developing a conscious partnership with your soul (Source energy within).

As you begin to reclaim your power, the Living in Alignment approach will assist you to develop a working understanding and skill base that facilitates

- ❖ living *authentically*
- ❖ *experiencing* enjoyment, happiness, courage, desire, connection, purpose, and fulfillment
- ❖ living up to your *full* potential
- ❖ manifesting *abundance* and love
- ❖ developing nurturing and deeply *satisfying* relationships
- ❖ experiencing *balance* and *harmony* in your life
- ❖ identifying and *meeting* both your human and soul needs
- ❖ *healing* from past and current traumatic experiences/wounding
- ❖ moving out of a *shame*- and/or fear-based reality
- ❖ developing a *conscious* connection with Source energy
- ❖ living an *inspired* life.

The Living in Alignment approach *meets* you where you are in your recovery process. Recognizing and acknowledging *where you are in your process* is one of the ways in which you own your reality. This doesn't mean that you have to *like* your situation. You are advised to *avoid* taking a one-up or one-down position when comparing yourself and your life with others; instead, view yourself and your life journey from the vantage point of *being different* rather than being better or worse. *Replace judgment with acceptance* of your position in life and all aspects of your reality. *The emphasis* is on illuminating the *significance* of each chapter in your life, and *not* on the problem, issue, challenge, or on what you don't want.

Living in Alignment encourages you to look upon and *experience 'mistakes' as learning opportunities*. Rather than focusing on mistakes, identifying and tuning into what is being *learned* is emphasized. Integrating these insights, gifts, and lessons into your behaviors is encouraged.

Living in Alignment will help you identify your *limiting beliefs and thinking* about yourself, your addiction and other conditions, living your life, other people, a power greater than your intellect, etc. You are offered a working understanding and skill base to help ensure that your mind is working in your best interests. Living in Alignment focuses on modifying, changing, or replacing limiting beliefs and ways of thinking with those that are *congruent* with the way Source energy works.

The Living in Alignment Model is *a holistic and preventative approach* in the treatment of substance abuse and substance/behavioral addictions. This integrative, whole-person approach works with your mind, body, heart, and spirit. This translates to identifying and addressing all aspects of your life, including your physical, emotional, behavioral, familial, spiritual, financial, social, educational, and psychological issues and accompanying challenges, problems, concerns, and needs.

The Living in Alignment approach *incorporates a combination of diverse modalities* such as cognitive-behavioral therapy, psycho-education, art therapy, body-centered psychotherapy, family systems, experiential work, life coaching, etc. A bio-psycho-socio-spiritual evaluation will identify your underlying issues that keep abuse and dependence in the driver's seat. A *customized treatment plan* is developed to meet your individual needs, challenges, developmental/emotional stages, issues, other conditions, and personal concerns. This will help ensure that the underlying causes that keep dependence in the driver's seat are addressed sufficiently and satisfactorily. Creating your customized treatment plan is a collaborative endeavor.

The Living in Alignment Approach to Recovery

❖ examines and works with both the literal reality and *symbolic* interpretation of abuse/dependence /relapse

❖ identifies and addresses your *unresolved* past and current issues and the *underlying causes* of your dependence

❖ *reframes* abuse/addiction/relapses as wake-up calls

❖ offers concepts to *expand* your awareness and ways of thinking about the significance of your life, a higher Power, all of your conditions, and their correlation to substance abuse/dependence

❖ is *heart-centered:* developed to assist you to open your heart to yourself, to others, and to living your life

❖ fosters developing a *spiritual practice* that is life-giving and life-sustainable

❖ facilitates living *authentically*

❖ assists people to *partner* with Source energy

❖ modifies or replaces *limiting* beliefs and ways of thinking

❖ is *customized* to meet individual needs, issues, concerns, challenges, etc.

❖ is *holistic* and preventative

❖ is *non-pathologizing* and non-stigmatizing

❖ offers a *skill base* to deal effectively with and manage your life on its terms

❖ fosters *self-empowerment*/healthy self-esteem

❖ cultivates becoming your own best friend and *ally*—coming to your rescue

❖ facilitates fulfilling your *calling* in life

❖ accelerates personal growth and *transformation*

Stages in Your Recovery

Because your uniqueness, which translates to having different needs, issues, challenges, and concerns, your ***treatment objectives, goals, and strategies will need to be individualized and customized***. Factors such as your age, ethnicity, sexual orientation, gender, economic status, social conditioning/expectations, educational background, cultural differences, religious and spiritual influences, and familial relationships will be taken into account to determine the best course of action in each stage of your recovery. Some of the most important factors that will determine the success of your treatment are

❖ your ***acceptance*** of your abuse/dependence

❖ your ***degree*** of receptivity/motivation to be in treatment

❖ your level of ***commitment*** to your recovery

❖ your level of cognitive ***functioning***.

The ***qualities*** that Living in Alignment fosters—determination, patience, the ability to delay gratification, perseverance, an attitude of gratitude, and a sense of humor—will help ensure that you ***thrive*** in your recovery.

Although there is no single *'right'* way to recover from addiction, the Living in Alignment Model identifies ***three stages*** in your recovery process. Within these stages are steps that people with substance abuse and addiction issues generally take. Having an understanding of these steps and the objectives involved will assist your mind/intellect to normalize and take down your defenses and be willing to enter into your recovery/healing process.

There are *three pre-stages* in your mental processing prior to beginning your recovery:

1. Awareness and Early Acknowledgment

This pre-stage position is marked by your growing awareness that *there is a problem*. This is often brought about by your family, friends, and coworkers or your health, financial, work, or legal problems and issues. Your awareness gradually turns into acknowledging that action is required, and shifting from *denying, avoiding, or minimizing* to being *willing* to change.

Although you may still be engaging in addictive behaviors and haven't made any measurable progress toward recovery, *this first step is critical* in paving the way for the rest of your recovery process.

2. Consideration

In this pre-stage position, you are *ready to take the first step* toward your recovery, often in the form of learning more about addiction and the impact it is having on your life and the lives of the people you care about.

3. Exploring Your Recovery

In this pre-stage position, you have moved past *denial*, are *motivated* to overcome your substance abuse/addiction, and are ***taking small steps*** such as exploring the concepts of moderation and abstinence. This is when you may ***attempt to control*** and/or ***try to stop*** your using behavior. This is also when you can make the critical ***decision*** to begin addiction treatment.

First Stage (Early) Recovery

During this stage your recovery focuses on detoxification and the management of your withdrawal symptoms; psycho-education around your abuse and dependence; psychiatric, medical, and psychological evaluations/testing; relapse prevention; identifying the underlying causes of your dependence; identifying and taking care of your basic needs; and providing suitable structure, support, and professional aftercare services. In early recovery you are ***vulnerable*** but are beginning to build the foundation for your new life. Some of the most important steps you can take during this stage are ***developing new coping skills and healthy habits*** and rebuilding damaged relationships.

Second Stage Recovery

During this stage your recovery focuses on your 'family of origin' issues; individuating and differentiating (becoming your own person); identifying and healing from unresolved trauma-related issues; identifying and healing your wounds of codependence (by learning essential life skills: learning to love yourself; learning to protect yourself; learning to own all aspects of your reality; learning to nurture yourself; and learning to live in moderation); modifying or replacing your limiting beliefs and thought patterns; integrating your newfound understanding and skills into your behaviors/lifestyle; your grief and loss issues; discovering/reclaiming your spirituality; and celebrating your new life of recovery.

Third Stage Recovery

During this stage your recovery focuses on learning to live authentically; finding meaning and purpose in your life and living up to your full potential; identifying fulfilling career and vocational choices; accelerating your personal transformation; and deepening your spirituality.

Living in Alignment emphasizes understanding the *reasons* for your substance abuse or addiction before attempting to *change* your behaviors.

Your needs, challenges, concerns, issues, shortcomings, and strengths are identified and prioritized in terms of their impact on your recovery/healing process. These stages of recovery overlap and, when working with professionals in the recovery field, are customized to meet you where you are in your recovery process.

The emotional and developmental delays caused by your using behavior are kept in the forefront when developing and implementing treatment goals/objectives. These goals are then broken down into manageable steps.

Living in Alignment *avoids labeling* and *pathologizing* as well as viewing your dependence as a *'problem'* to be solved. Rather, the focus is on identifying and working through the *underlying causes* that are keeping your dependence in the driver's seat. In addition, you are offered the skill base to embody *a transformational presence* that is about being *very loving, very accepting, and very patient* with yourself.

Living in Alignment offers you a sense of hope for a better life: that possibilities abound; and that your recovery is *intended* as a springboard to a *new beginning*, offering a promise of fulfillment that is within your grasp.

Your Reasons For Using

If you have substance abuse/addiction, ask yourself: *'What keeps dependence in the driver's seat?'* If you want to thrive in your recovery, it will be necessary to identify and understand the reasons why you began using in the first place, and why you continued to use.

Your addiction is not the problem. It is the underlying *causes* that keep you dependent on substances and on behaviors. Below are some of the most common reasons why people use. Check ☑ the ones that apply to you.

☐ fears/anxiety

☐ covering up emotional pain (grief and loss)

☐ hopelessness

- [ ] heartache
- [ ] traumas (PTSD symptoms)
- [ ] sexual, emotional, psychological, physical abuse
- [ ] humiliation
- [ ] betrayal
- [ ] having low self esteem/hating or not liking yourself and/or your life
- [ ] living in a shame-based reality
- [ ] relief
- [ ] let-downs
- [ ] 'victim consciousness'
- [ ] self-pity
- [ ] inability to deal with life on its terms
- [ ] problems, issues, challenges, worries
- [ ] shortcomings
- [ ] self-medicating a mood or anxiety condition
- [ ] to escape from some aspect of your reality/life
- [ ] to continue to avoid and/or live in denial about something
- [ ] to be cool/fit in with your peer group
- [ ] to expand your consciousness
- [ ] to feel good
- [ ] to manage physical pain

- ☐ to block disturbing memories
- ☐ to suppress your appetite
- ☐ to feel energized
- ☐ to feel uninhibited
- ☐ to feel more comfortable in your body
- ☐ to numb out from self-deprecating self-talk
- ☐ to avoid feeling certain emotions
- ☐ to cope with your life
- ☐ to expand your mind
- ☐ to open your heart
- ☐ to attempt to access your authentic self
- ☐ to experience bliss
- ☐ to fill a void/emptiness
- ☐ to hide from yourself and the world
- ☐ to boost a poor self-image
- ☐ to deal with an inferiority complex
- ☐ to self-medicate ADD
- ☐ to avoid problems
- ☐ as a crutch to change ordinary everyday reality from unbearable to bearable
- ☐ to avoid withdrawal symptoms
- ☐ to manage stress

The *personal characteristics* that typically underlie *addiction* are:

❖ poor *self-regulation*;

❖ a lack of basic *differentiation*;

❖ a lack of a healthy *sense of self*;

❖ a sense of deficiency and *emptiness*;

❖ impaired *impulse control*.

U SING Behavior
Here, standing in front of the mirror,
        looking at my reflection,
gazing into my eyes as if they were a bottomless chasm,
with the exactitude of kaleidoscopic intensity I see...

        the fathomless pit of illusion, deception, and lies

        the dead end of despair

        the mercilessness of self-deprecation

        the depths of depression

        the self-delusion of denial

        the anguish and terror of being lost forever

        the agony of self-defeat

        the despair of self-abandonment.

Emerging from the dazed and confused state
        of being in a maze,
coming out of the fog of my last high,
and forced into facing the truth of my reality...

Benefits of the LIA Approach to Recovery

Here is a list of some of the most noteworthy benefits of Living in Alignment. You will begin to experience these benefits as soon as you start saying *'Yes!'* to you and your life, get off the recovery fence, and commit to and be proactive about your recovery/healing process.

- ❖ *become your own person* (individuate/ differentiate)
- ❖ *live authentically* (access/speak/live in your truth)
- ❖ *open your heart* to yourself and to your life
- ❖ gain the *skill base* to form satisfying/nurturing relationships
- ❖ become *self-empowered*
- ❖ engage in activities, lifestyle, people, organizations, behaviors, and diet that are *life-giving/life-sustaining*
- ❖ discover your *life calling/soul mission*
- ❖ become familiar with and work through *life themes/challenges*
- ❖ know that *you are deeply loved*
- ❖ start living up to *your greatest potential*
- ❖ become receptive to *change*
- ❖ experience healthy *self-esteem*
- ❖ experience *more* fun, spontaneity, passion, joy

❖ discover an abiding sense of *peace and serenity*

❖ experience *balance and harmony*

❖ integrate essential *life skills* into your behaviors

❖ be able to hold yourself *accountable* and take responsibility for your life

❖ have *the courage to question* the status quo and find your own voice

❖ be able to *Trust* (yield to) and *Surrender* to (merge with) Source energy and the unfolding of your life

Some of the Skills You'll Develop

The Living in Alignment approach to recovery will teach you a skill base to regulate and balance your energy. *Developing a partnership with your soul* is an effective (if not the *most* effective) approach to balancing your energy in ways that are life-giving and life-sustaining.

Partnering with your soul is *simple* in both theory and practice. In short, it is about listening to and following the prompting of your soul—the deepest, most intimate aspect of who you are. The guidance being offered to your mind/human self is tapping into *your truth* and the wisdom of the universe or *Consciousness itself*.

Some of the *skills you will learn* by Living in Alignment are

- ❖ identifying and meeting *your needs*
- ❖ developing effective *communication skills* with yourself and others
- ❖ learning to listen to and follow the *guidance* and prompting from your soul
- ❖ recognizing and acknowledging that all of the circumstances in your past, present, and future are *integral* to your personal growth
- ❖ developing a *spiritual practice* that is life-giving and life-sustaining
- ❖ establishing and maintaining *functional boundaries*
- ❖ modifying, changing, replacing your *limiting beliefs*/ways of thinking
- ❖ *reclaiming your power* from dependence, other people, events, limiting beliefs
- ❖ developing beliefs that are *congruent* with universal principles
- ❖ becoming *process-oriented* (being able to track your mind/intellect)
- ❖ becoming *emotionally available* to yourself and others
- ❖ working directly with consciousness (becoming adept at *manifesting* your purpose)
- ❖ developing your *presence/awareness* and integrating your *mindfulness* skills
- ❖ *regulating* your energy (how you feel mentally, emotionally, physically)

9

Will I be able to use substances again?

THE short answer is: *probably not*. Maintaining *complete abstinence* from alcohol and addictive drugs will be necessary, based on the fact that these substances have an *addictive quality*, particularly for people who have become dependent upon them. Because of this it is paramount that you keep in the forefront that *it can take only one use* (of whatever addictive substance) to reactivate your brain chemistry, which will more than likely lead you directly back to becoming dependent.

Research findings into brain mapping show that the reward center in the cerebral frontal cortex of your brain lights up when exposed to stimuli (memories, thoughts, places, people, behaviors, events) associated with your past using behaviors.

These studies have confirmed that your habits (such as using behavior) and the brain circuits that maintain them form around substances and behaviors that promise instant (if temporary) satisfaction.

Once these habit structures are formed in your nervous system, they will likely guide your behavior without free choice.

As a result, individuals with abuse and addiction will *value* the addictive substance or behavior and *undervalue* the healthy alternative.

Repeated drug use leads to long-lasting changes in your brain that **undermine** voluntary control.

In the center of your forehead in the front part of your brain lies the **ventral medial prefrontal cortex** that takes in information, sorts it out, and decides what action to take. **Alcohol and drug abuse/addiction** can and does cause this area of your brain to malfunction. If this part of your cortex is impaired or poorly developed before your addiction takes hold, it will be further damaged by your drug use.

Malfunctioning brain circuitry may override your rational judgment and intention. This plays out in making foolish and potentially fatal decisions (excessive risk-taking behaviors, driving while intoxicated, reacting instead of responding, making impulsive decisions, etc.).

The good news is that after you have been away from addictive drugs, your ventral medial prefrontal cortex **will begin functioning properly again** (this varies from person to person) instead of causing you to make decisions that are harmful to you and undermine your goals and best intentions.

When you experience stressors/aspects of your reality that you have difficulty being with, accepting, and/or working through, you will have difficulty refraining from using. Your 'reality' refers to what is happening to you mentally, emotionally, physically, and intuitively, along with your behaviors.

You may have difficulty owing some (or all) aspects of your reality. Instead of identifying and accepting these, and learning skills to live life on its terms, you may use mind-altering drugs to escape, numb out, hide from, or otherwise suppress aspects of your reality, including

❖ your *emotional* reality, such as fear, anger, shame, guilt, emotional pain

❖ your *mental* reality, such as worries, concerns, unresolved issues, stressors, or mental conditions

❖ your *physical* reality, such as physical pain and medical conditions

❖ your *spiritual* reality, such as not listening to and/or following your intuition if you don't like what your intuition is guiding/prompting you to say or do

❖ your *behavioral* reality, such as not wanting to (or being able to) hold yourself accountable and be responsible for what is happening in your life and the consequences of your using behaviors

When you experience any *stimuli* linked to your using behavior (people, places, or things), or your *triggers* for using (being stressed, restless, overwhelmed, lonely, upset, bored, angry, or in physical or emotional pain), you will be in danger of *relapsing* unless you establish a new *default response* that challenges your triggers.

These triggers and stimuli will *no longer pose a threat*—and can actually help you deepen in your recovery—when you learn to *recognize* them and *choose* more appropriate thinking and behavior. Identifying and working through the *issues underlying your triggers* is the key to discovering your new *'freedom to choose'*.

Living in Alignment does *not* claim to offer a *cure* for your addiction. I do, however, concur with others in the recovery field that a *complete remission of dependence* is possible once the *underlying causes* are identified and sufficiently addressed.

Living in Alignment will accelerate your personal growth and ensure sustainable transformation by assisting you to develop a working understanding and skill base to partner effectively with your soul.

To reiterate, your *cravings, desires, and urges to use will greatly diminish* once you have identified and sufficiently addressed, worked through, and healed the underlying causes that drove you to drink alcohol and/or use addictive drugs in the first place. In other words, you will no longer crave those substances to self-medicate those underlying causes.

As your connection with your soul deepens, your insecurities, confusion, unease, distrust, cynicism, doubts, ambivalence, uncertainty, misgivings, and the like about living in your physical body will be replaced with an abiding sense of contentment, acceptance, belonging, serenity, and zest for living.

In the process of identifying and addressing the underlying causes of your dependence, you will begin *feeling good* physically, mentally, and emotionally without the need to use alcohol and addictive drugs. As you deepen in your recovery, you will experience a happy, fulfilling, and substance-free life without the *fear of relapse*.

If you do *not* identify and sufficiently work through the underlying causes that are keeping your *dependence* in the driver's seat, you will tend to *swap addictions*. You may be able to stop using your drug of choice, but then begin using another psychotropic drug to which you weren't previously addicted. When this happens, your new drug with addictive qualities opens up the reward center of your brain and can become a *gateway drug* that leads you back to using your drug of choice in a vicious cycle.

Once you stop using addictive substances, it is common to develop *a process/behavioral addiction* like shopping/spending, gambling, compulsive sex, eating, or working long hours. Again I want to point out that *the problem is not the dependence itself*, but the failure to identify and/or sufficiently address the underlying causes.

W E are all butterflies.
Earth is our chrysalis.
—LeeAnn Taylor

MY Declaration of Self-Esteem

I am me.
  In all of the world,
  there is no one else exactly like me.
  There are persons who have some parts like me.
  But no one adds up exactly like me.
  Therefore, everything that comes out of me
  is authentically mine
  because I alone chose it.

I OWN everything about me...
  my body, including everything it does;
  my mind, including all of its thoughts and ideas;
  my eyes, including the images of all they behold;
  my feelings, whatever they may be...
  anger, joy, frustration, love, disappointment, excitement;
  my mouth, and all the words that come out of it,
  polite, sweet, or rough, correct or incorrect;
  my voice, loud or soft;
  and all my actions,
  whether they be to others or to myself.

I OWN my fantasies, my dreams, my hopes, my fears.
  I own my triumphs and successes,
  all my failures and mistakes.
  Because I own all of me,
  I can become intimately acquainted with me.
  By so doing I can love me
  and be friendly with me in all my parts;
  I can then make it possible for all of me
  to work in my best interests.

I KNOW there are aspects about myself
that puzzle me,
and other aspects that I do not know.
But as long as I am friendly
and loving to myself,
I can courageously and hopefully look
for the solutions to the puzzles
and for ways to find out
more about me.
However I look and sound,
whatever I say and do,
and whatever I think and feel
at a given moment in time
is me.

THIS is authentic and represents
where I am at that moment in time.
When I review later
how I looked and sounded,
what I said and did,
and how I thought and felt,
some parts may turn out to be unfitting.
I can discard that which is unfitting,
and keep that which proved fitting,
and invent something new
for that which I discarded.

I CAN see, hear, feel, think, say, and do.
I have the tools to survive,
to be close to others,
to be productive,
and to make sense and order
out of the world of people
and things outside of me.

—Virginia Satir

PART TWO

THE remaining chapters of this book explore in depth various themes of the Living in Alignment approach that were introduced in previous chapters.

Having both an intellectual grasp of these concepts and being receptive to the Living in Alignment perspective will *increase* your understanding and awareness, help you *challenge* any misconceptions, and *open your mind* to the possibilities that await you in your recovery.

Gaining a working understanding of these themes will assist your mind/intellect in *replacing your mental defenses* with an acknowledgment of the importance of developing a *conscious partnership* with your soul (Source energy within).

You may have very *limiting, rigid, and detrimental beliefs and views about spirituality* in general, and even less awareness and understanding of its *pertinence* to your recovery and your life.

Developing a *conscious partnership* with your soul will prove to be the most rewarding and life-changing experience you can imagine. Having a *conscious connection* with your spiritual nature will ensure that *thriving in your recovery* becomes your new reality.

WE do not see things as they are; we see things as *we* are.
—The Talmud

10

Opening Your Heart to Recovery

YOUR recovery and transformation begin with opening your heart. If you have struggled for years to overcome self-sabotaging and self-hating behaviors, *opening your heart* is your first step in deciding to say '*Yes!*' to you and your life. It is the key to *sustaining* your recovery. It will illuminate your true desires and access the deepest truth of who you are.

Here are the main points explored in this chapter. I encourage you to entertain these concepts from the perspective of '*What if it is true?*' Check ☑ those that are most significant for your recovery or that you have questions or concerns about.

☐ An open heart counteracts your *negative* self-talk (shaming messages).

☐ An open heart will assist you to suspend *judgments* of yourself and others.

☐ An open heart helps you to *forgive*.

☐ An open heart keeps you *self-empowered*.

☐ An open heart fosters *healthy* relationships.

☐ An open heart releases you from *your past*.

☐ An open heart accesses the *healer* within.

☐ An open heart offers a direct *connection* to Source energy.

☐ An open heart frees you from ***victim consciousness***.

☐ An open heart removes you from fear- and ***shame-based*** realities.

☐ An open heart will assist you to maintain ***balance and harmony*** in your life.

ALICE in Wonderland
Down the rabbit hole picking up speed
the earth smells damp and rooty.

Nothing to hang onto in the dark,
I become smaller and smaller as I drift towards the core.

    Tears of desperation fall from my face
    as I wait for the bottom,
    I can no longer feel ten feet tall.

No one sees me, no one hears me cry out,
Smaller and smaller, my voice cannot be heard.

    I choke with dirt in my mouth,
    soon I will disappear forever lost.
    I cannot lose my head
    like the queen of hearts said.

I awoke from this dream still tasting dirt in my mouth.
That was the moment I reclaimed my life,

The miracle came as I awoke from desperation.
The journey of recovery began.

Alice in Wonderland *is my beginning in recovery.* My Forgiveness [page 116] *is the discovery of healing and love and discovery of the woman that I was always meant to be, love, my awakening into recovery, and the last,* Mt Everest [page 136] *is the continued journey of letting go of past fears.*

—Joanna Shaw

COULD it be that we are intended to give and receive love in all of our interactions? Many years ago I began noticing the qualitative difference between having an open heart instead of a closed one. I found that opening your heart is *the most effective means to access Source energy*, which is love. Your heart is the universal symbol representing *the direct pathway to Source energy.*

Learning to keep your heart open is one of the most effective transformational strategies available. It is simple in practice and often has profound results. Some of the more common qualities of an open heart are *understanding, patience, gentleness, forgiveness, generosity, compassion, respect, kindness, empathy,* and *caring.* The most pronounced quality of an open heart is *love.* When we are loving, the energy of love permeates our entire being.

The Importance of Love

Having an open heart and intending to access your truth will assist you to transform your story. You can avoid getting caught up in the mundane aspects of the 'drama' you have created in your daily life and focus on what is most important: how all of your experiences are intended to facilitate living up to your greatest potential.

An open heart is the pathway to your soul (Source energy within). When you open your heart, you open the door to Source energy. If you want to keep this door open, it is necessary to keep your mind/human self from getting in the way.

We all want to know that we are loved. In the Living in Alignment process you will discover that not only are you deeply loved, but *at your essence you* **are** *love*.

When you love, you put aside differences. Love will assist you to **suspend** your judgments as well as to **release** your resentments. Why? Because when you open your heart, you increase your energy. This higher energy **removes mental defenses** and opens your mind to see *'the bigger picture'* of your life.

When this occurs you will see and relate to everyone's humanity and spirituality. Your soul will illuminate the **significance** of your human life, normalize your imperfections, and call your attention to the possibilities available within all of your interactions and relationships.

Love energy is the elixir of life. It is the best feel-good energy available, and better yet, it is free. It releases endorphins in your brain. It is the best *'high'* available. Better still, it has no adverse side effects. All that is required is to focus on and develop your capacity to experience love by radiating love outward as well as to yourself. In other words, this entails both **giving** and **receiving love.**

When you open your heart **everything begins to change**. An open heart **can** change your mood, your attitude, your thoughts, and your behavior. I say *'can'* because you will need to couple an open heart with an **open mind** to facilitate personal change.

Developing your capacity to receive love begins with *loving yourself.* When you love yourself, you raise your energy to the level of *love—the highest energy.* Being loving keeps you focused on experiencing more enjoyment, happiness, vitality, passion, and connection in your life. Love is the medium through which your soul communicates with your mind.

Your human self/intellect needs a lot of *tender loving care* the moment you choose to be proactive about coming to your own rescue and getting your life together. Accessing the qualities of an open heart is necessary to facilitate this process. Once your human self recognizes the *all-important qualities* of an open heart, it becomes easier to discern which quality (understanding, generosity, kindness, forgiveness, patience, gentleness, etc.) is required in your daily interactions with yourself and others.

An Open Heart is Healing

Having your heart open also serves to *release healing energy.* This energy goes to whatever aspect of your human self needs healing and does what is needed to facilitate your healing.

Your healing may take different forms, such as

❖ your *recognition* that you can modify, replace, or discard a limiting belief

❖ your *strength* to change a damaging behavior

❖ your *insight* and impetus to bring about an emotional release

❖ your *clarity* to change or move out of a damaging relationship dynamic

❖ your *courage* to face your fears

❖ your *wherewithal* to come to your own rescue

❖ your *decision* to hold yourself accountable and take responsibility for your life.

These mental and emotional shifts have a direct impact on healing your *physical conditions*.

It is *not your responsibility* to ensure that people receive the love you offer. Do not lose any sleep if others are not willing or able to receive (or give) love. It is difficult to witness this, let alone remain neutral. When you are not Living in Alignment with your soul, your human self can easily get caught up in your mind's limiting conditioning, becoming *reactive* and taking things too personally.

Encountering your unconscious *'shadow'* aspects is a sign that your human self is getting in your way. Negativity, skewed thinking, addictions, and other things about yourself or your life you dislike or don't want to own may indicate that *your heart is closed*, that a release of your emotional *'baggage'* is occurring, or that *healing* is in progress.

You can develop your awareness to become adept at seeing that *everything* occurring in your life is intended to provide maximum benefit. When you are experiencing *difficult* or *disowned* aspects of your reality, this becomes your cue to keep your heart open to receive their benefits and continue offering love to yourself.

Being *an exemplar* by having your heart open is the most effective method of teaching others how to love and keep their hearts open as well.

Loving Yourself and Others

It may be easier for you to love others than to love yourself. You may have been taught the importance of loving others while at the same time being told that loving yourself is bad, wrong, or even sinful. You may give the excuse that loving yourself is selfish, self-centered, and self-seeking. Dysfunction ensues when you live in the extremes of *giving without receiving* love or vice versa.

When you only give and do not receive love, *you deplete your energy.* This often presents as *physical exhaustion, depression, anger, mental confusion,* etc. When you give without receiving love, you invariably *become resentful.* Likewise, when you only receive and do not give love, you become *self-centered.*

When you love others but not yourself, you will tend to offer *conditional love* that has *strings attached*: you expect something in return every time! Love is intended to be freely given. This can happen only when your heart is full, so to speak.

WHERE you stumble,
there lies your treasure.
— Joseph Campbell

Developing Your Capacity to Love

You develop the capacity to give love freely by giving and receiving love. When your energy is depleted, you have no love to give. You want to hide under the covers. This is an attempt to replenish your energy, and is in order if it includes giving yourself a lot of *tender loving care* (identifying and taking care of your needs).

You may be caught up in *dysfunctional* interpersonal behavioral patterns: you keep giving until you are hovering on the edge of burnout. You keep on going, but just barely, and look like death warmed over. Your overall performance is mediocre at best. The more your energy gets depleted, the more likely you are setting yourself up for physical, mental, and emotional stress that can *trigger a relapse* or lead to illnesses and all sorts of conditions.

When you are loving yourself as well as loving others, you come from a place of abundance. When you love yourself, you naturally go about tending to your needs. When you love others and do not love yourself sufficiently, you'll tend to *prioritize* other people's needs and not your own. Neglecting your needs is a form of *self-abandonment*. When you do not attend to your needs, you have *less energy* to love others and yourself. You also have less energy to live your life.

I EXPECT nothing.
I fear nothing. I am free.
— Nikos Kazantzakis [epitaph]

Love, Self-sacrifice, and Narcissism

Narcissism is the grandiose belief that the world revolves around you and your conditions. You may become overly focused on yourself and your needs and wants as a result of childhood wounding that is exacerbated by your substance or process addictions.

Neglecting your basic human needs *blocks* or interferes with your experience of *enjoyment, happiness, balance, passion, energy, power, connection, satisfaction, and fulfillment.* When you become too focused on another person's needs, you *believe* his/her needs are more important than your own. (This does not apply to dependents who are incapable of taking care of themselves.) When you prioritize the needs of others and neglect your own, you will tend to place *unrealistic expectations* on others. You'll expect them to read your mind, know what your needs are, and/or take care of your needs.

When you receive love without giving love, you will feel disconnected from others and yourself. Why? Because when you focus only on yourself, you become self-absorbed.

We are all *interconnected* and *interdependent*. When you forget this truth, the result is imbalance and *unnecessary suffering*. The middle ground is *interdependence*. This is about finding the right balance between giving and receiving love in all of your interactions. Believe it or not, *we all need love*, whether or not you are aware of it.

Enough Is Enough!

You have reached a *crossroads in your life* when you acknowledge you have closed your heart, feel the *damage, grief, and loss*, and *desire* to open your heart. Realizing that *enough is enough,* you are ready to make a *once-and-for-all decision*. You acknowledge that closing your heart to yourself, to others, and to life is *no longer an option*. This is when you declare to yourself and to the world that *from here on out, you will keep your heart open.*

❖ No matter how many *mistakes* you make,

❖ no matter if you are *penniless*,

❖ no matter if your partner has *cheated* on you,

❖ no matter if you have been *abused* or *abusive* to others or yourself

❖ no matter if you think you have *ruined* other people's lives or your own,

❖ no matter if *injustices* prevail,

❖ no matter if you *think* you or others are not worthy of love,

❖ no matter if you've been *neglected*, *abandoned*, or *betrayed*,

❖ no matter if *cruelty* continues in the world,

❖ no matter if you have been *let down* continuously,

❖ no matter if you have *relapsed* time and time again,

❖ no matter if all seems *lost*,

❖ no matter *what* —

you make a commitment to keep your heart open.

Whenever you recognize that you have *closed* your heart to yourself, to others, to life, or to living your life, you can renew this pledge.

The act of opening your heart is a *transformer* of energy. It is the one action you can take that *will always have a positive impact* on yourself and your life, as well as on others and their lives. Although it may not always be immediate (for various reasons), opening your heart will *always* have a *favorable* result. Always, always, always. No exceptions! Try it. If your heart is already open, you are resonating with these words. If your heart is closed, you may be experiencing some *resistance*. The good news is that you can learn to open your heart, and if it is already open, you can learn to open it even more.

Wounding, Resentments, and Forgiveness

When you look back at your *wounding*, especially any wounding that was the result of abuse (your own or others'), the best medicine is to keep your heart open to everyone. Love serves as a healing salve to your wounding. Even if it is difficult to keep your heart open, you can still *keep an intention* to open your heart.

You are *not* going to do this perfectly. Whenever there has been wounding, it is probable that you will be resentful. *Holding onto resentments* is a sure way to keep your heart closed to yourself and others. On an energetic level, your unwillingness or inability to release resentments keeps you living in shackles. The key to releasing resentments is to learn how to *forgive* yourself and others.

Being human means making mistakes, even when you put your best foot forward. Hopefully you will allow your mistakes to become learning opportunities. When you *forgive* someone, you are acknowledging your own humanness and *imperfections*. Forgiving does *not* mean forgetting or living in denial about what transpired. It does mean *being no longer obsessed* about a mistake and no longer using that as *ammunition* against the person who made the mistake (including yourself).

The act of forgiveness is intended to release you from *resentments, bitterness, animosity, antagonism, and the like*. Many people are caught up in an-eye-for-an-eye mentality. This perpetuates doing the same things we detest in others.

Forgiveness is as much *for you* as it is for the one you are forgiving. It is *not until you truly forgive* that you can move forward with your life and allow others to do the same. Forgiveness is not only a quality of an open heart, but also a practice and a process that can actually *reopen* a closed heart.

The Role of Your Mind in Opening Your Heart

The Living in Alignment process involves *de-programming* and *reprogramming* your mind. An integral part of this process is *examining your beliefs*. It involves *identifying* your beliefs, *discerning* their origin, and *understanding* how they shape your character, behavior, choices, decisions, and interactions (with yourself, with others, with Source energy, and with life).

The good news is that you can *modify* or *change* what you come to discern as *limiting* or undesirable beliefs, perceptions, attitudes, behaviors, and expectations. This requires time and all the qualities of an open heart.

Opening your heart allows wisdom from Source energy to speak *through* you. As this occurs, you gain access to the possibilities and opportunities available within any given situation. You also gain awareness of what is required of you to integrate this knowledge into your life.

Love is *essential* to your health and wellbeing. To experience its wondrous effects, you will need to *develop your capacity both to give and to receive love*. Your human self/intellect is the vehicle for consciousness to work through you. For example, when you are about to say something to and/or do something for another or for yourself, you can ask yourself, 'Is what I am about to say or do *unifying or divisive*?' If your answer is *divisive*, it is an indication that your heart is closed and a cue to open it again.

Loving Yourself Unconditionally

Your human self needs a lot of loving attention in order to change or modify your limited or unwanted conditioning. You will learn to develop *a loving relationship with all aspects of your human self.* You will need this new experience to remove your mental defenses and promote your healing.

The Living in Alignment process does not force; it *invites*. Aggression produces fear, and you do *not* want to instill more fear in your mind. Your heart energy has a soothing impact on your mind and your human self. Thus challenging your mind *with your heart open* is both important and necessary.

The Living in Alignment process is about *learning to love yourself unconditionally and live from this place*. Establishing a loving relationship with yourself becomes a priority. The more you are Living in Alignment, the more loving you become to yourself as well as to others.

Our Present Situation on Planet Earth

This is a time of great shifting on Planet Earth. In this transitional period it's important that you *respond in love* rather than *react* to the *'madness'* occurring all around us. Remember that to a lesser or greater extent *chaos* is an inherent component of any transformational process. You do not have one without the other.

Opening your heart and radiating love to others as well as to yourself will assist you in *establishing and maintaining balance and harmony in your life.* Do not let your mind (with its limiting conditioning) convince you to keep your heart closed. Any and all of the reasons to close your heart (including your *obsessive reactions*) are irrelevant, and are a clue that your human self is in *fear mode.* All your reasons to keep your heart closed become *excuses* for *NOT*

❖ living up to your *greatest potential*

❖ *acknowledging* Source energy

❖ claiming your *power* and the experiences you are intended to have

❖ taking full *responsibility* for your life

❖ *experiencing* contentment, serenity, passion, and happiness

❖ accomplishing your *calling in life* and experiencing *soul fulfillment.*

The choice to open or close your heart in all of your interactions is *yours to make* every second of every day.

G OD doesn't close one door
without opening a better one ~
BUT ~ we've got to get our fingers
out of the closing door.
The reason you're in pain is because
you have your fingers in a door
God is trying to close.

Practices to open your heart and/or keep it open

1. Be *intimate* with yourself (consciously choose to be your own best friend and ally).

2. Live and let live (follow your dreams and *encourage* others to do the same).

3. Practice suspending *judgment*.

4. Teach love by *offering* it.

5. Genuinely *compliment* yourself and others often.

6. Get in the habit of asking yourself if your intentions are *unifying* or *divisive*.

7. Practice creating a loving *presence*, both when alone and in the company of others.

8. Carry an object with you to remind yourself of some quality of an open heart that you want to *integrate* into all aspects of your life.

9. Praise and *reward* yourself and others often.

10. Normalize the fact that a loving relationship *takes time*.

11. Continually communicate with yourself about ways to keep your heart *open to everyone*.

12. Unplug from the *illusion* of perfectionism. (Remember, no one is perfect.)

13. Practice an attitude of *gratitude*.

14. Keep saying '*Yes!*' to yourself and to life.

15. Be of *service* to others.

16. *Exemplify* the qualities of an open heart.

11

Discovering Your Spirituality

ABUSE of every kind has a spiritual component: something profound within you is violated. Believe it or not, deny it or not, love it or hate it, your *core reality* feels assaulted. Recovering your personal sense of your *spiritual integrity* is essential to saying *'Yes!'* to you and your life.

The sense of emptiness and *angst* you may experience early in your recovery comes from feeling *disconnected* from your spiritual nature. Remember that you are *both* a spiritual *and* a human being, *not* one or the other. The two are inseparable. When you *overemphasize* one and *deny* or *neglect* the other, you create imbalance and disharmony.

You may be *unaware* of this vital connection, have a *limiting* understanding of it, or *fear* or *disown* it. The process of becoming your own person is key to living authentically, and can be truly realized *only* by embracing your spirituality.

Here are the main points explored in this chapter. I encourage you to entertain these concepts from the perspective of *'What if it is true?'* Check ☑ those that are most significant for your recovery or that you have questions or concerns about.

☐ We are *all* spiritual beings.

☐ Spirituality is the practice of resourcing yourself from your *soul*.

☐ Spirituality is the act of both recognizing and acknowledging that you are a *spiritual* being.

☐ Spirituality is about acknowledging that in essence you are *equal* to everyone else and that your presence on Planet Earth is of *significance*.

☐ Spirituality is about soul *realization* (acknowledging that on the deepest level of your being you are a unique reflection of Source energy).

☐ Spirituality is about soul *actualization* (living up to your greatest potential).

☐ Spirituality is about *acknowledging* that you have your own life to live.

☐ Spirituality is what happens when you begin living your life by listening to and following the *prompting* of your soul.

☐ Spirituality is about claiming your *birthright* to be living in your physical body, living on Planet Earth, and having your own life.

I N everyone's life,
there is a journey difficult to undertake —
daunting in every way measurable —
but necessary for one's spirit to be honored,
one's destiny to be fulfilled.

—Lao-Tzu

W E are spiritual beings first and foremost. You do not need to learn how to become spiritual because *you are spiritual*. Does this make sense to you? Spiritual can be viewed as synonymous with sacred, and in reality all of life is sacred!

As a unique reflection of Source energy, you are one with Source energy. Because we are all from the same source, we are interconnected. Thus at the level of your soul *you are equal to, not less than or better than* other people.

Spirituality versus Religion

Recovering your sense of *being grounded in your spirituality* is complicated by the uneasy or confusing relationships many people have with traditional religious practices.

Religion and spirituality are not mutually exclusive, but neither are they one and the same. The main difference is that *religion is usually associated with an organization* (along with dogma), while spirituality is not. As a spiritual being *you may or may not choose* to be affiliated with a religious organization, but if you are religious, you most likely will be.

Many people think of spirituality as *synonymous* with religion, and because of this have inadvertently and unknowingly attempted to *disconnect* from their spirituality because *they don't want anything to do with religion*.

Many people have walked away from **religious organizations** or want **nothing** to do with them. Here are some of the most common reasons people make the decision to leave religious organizations or choose **non-affiliation**. Check ☑ any concerns that may apply to you.

☐ fear of becoming (or feeling you have been) **brainwashed**

☐ not believing the **dogma** these organizations espouse or impose

☐ disagreeing with the **stances** these organizations take

☐ the apparent **hypocrisy**

☐ the **lies**, deceit, and misconceptions perpetuated by religious organizations

☐ the **wars** that have been waged in the name of God and the subsequent **atrocities**

☐ what often appears to be **misguided** leadership

☐ the **sexual abuse** endemic within religious organizations

☐ the **misuse** and abuse of power and authority

☐ the psychological, emotional, and spiritual **abuse** that leaders of organizations have inflicted upon people

☐ the inability to respond effectively to the **spiritual** needs of their congregants.

The reasons people walk away from religious organizations are *valid, justified,* and at times a *necessary step* to heal and prevent any further assaults on their sensibilities. Behind these reasons for leaving are a trail of unresolved emotional, psychological, and spiritual issues and *impairment.*

Your *spirituality* is what connects your human self with your deepest core: your soul. It is an integral and essential aspect of who you are. By attempting to *deny* or *disown* the existence or the significance of your spirituality, you are cutting yourself off from Source energy—your life force!

Ignoring, denying, minimizing, or *downplaying* the significance of your spirituality are ways in which you *abandon* yourself, creating *discord* between your human self and your soul that results in a lack of meaning and purpose in your life.

People who are spiritual *may be called* (as part of their soul mission) to be associated with religious organizations, but from a place of *being a transformative presence* within those organizations in order to *raise* awareness, *deepen* people's understanding, and *assist* in bringing about change.

Many people who are religious think *they need an intermediary* to access Source energy.

People who *acknowledge* that they are spiritual beings know that *they can access Source energy directly* without the need for any sort of go-between. As a spiritual being you have access to the wisdom of Universal Mind at any time, anywhere, and in any place. You can just as easily connect with Source energy in nature, in meditation, in your dream state, doing yoga, eating delicious food, taking in beauty, etc., as in a church, synagogue, or mosque.

Partnering with Source Energy

Ultimately *you are a spiritual being having a human experience* or learning how it is to be human.

Your spirituality is also about being in relationship with Source energy. As your awareness increases, so too will your understanding that *you are co-creating your reality*. This is the practice of partnering with Source energy. Believe it or not, *you are always co-creating with Source energy*—consciously or not. You can become *conscious* of how you partner with this energy, and thus more skilled at co-creating your reality in your daily living.

Living in Alignment facilitates the key skills of developing your presence and awareness and training your mind to defer to your soul by listening to and following your intuition.

Living in Your Truth

Your spirituality is *the practice of 'being' in the world*. In this context 'being' refers to living from or resourcing yourself from your soul. This is about *living in the truth of who you are* and what you have come here to do.

Your truth will be *hidden* as long as you are primarily *externally resourced* (believing that you are only your human self and that the three-dimensional world you see is all there is) and live your life based upon *societal dictates* (how others want or expect you to live). In this context you lose contact with your soul or *who you really are*.

When you are being spiritual you are *internally resourced:* listening to your intuition (the voice of your soul) and following its prompting.

Being *internally resourced* involves *feeling into* your life instead of trying to *figure out* your life (by relying on being *externally resourced*). Initially this may be difficult for your mind to grasp, but it will make sense as your human self becomes more internally resourced.

Your spirituality is the practice of living your life, specifically *listening to and following the guidance and prompting from your soul.* The Living in Alignment approach will assist you both to access your intuition and to discover your internal resources (your soul connection).

You are living *authentically* when you are Living in Alignment with your soul. This means being your *unique* self: different from every other being and at the same time connected with all life forms.

Grounding Your Spirituality

It is essential to ground your spirituality *in your physical reality*. Otherwise you will tend to deny, avoid, escape, minimize, and neglect your human responsibilities (known as *spiritual bypassing*). You can *avoid* spiritual bypassing by *remaining present* in your daily living while utilizing your awareness and mindfulness skills.

This is where *owning all aspects* of your reality (mental, emotional, physical, spiritual, behaviors, and your actual experiencing) come into play, along with identifying and working through your issues, concerns, and challenges and taking full responsibility for all aspects of your life.

The Living in Alignment approach will teach you to be *solution-focused* as well as to look for *opportunities* in all the life circumstances in which you may find yourself. A grounded spirituality will help you

❖ *maintain* balance and harmony in your life

❖ meet *both* your human and soul needs

❖ *deepen* in all of your relationships

❖ live up to your *full* potential

❖ access your *truth*

❖ *evolve* in love, enjoyment, serenity, passion, connection, satisfaction, and happiness

Meaning, Purpose, and Living from your Soul

Your soul knows what it is here for, and that your life has *meaning and purpose*. You have a *soul mission* or calling in life. It is your *birthright* to discover what your soul mission is along with living out or completing it, which is what leads to *soul fulfillment*. You can view your spirituality as the practice of fully living your life by accomplishing your soul mission.

This is about *experiencing everything that your soul has come into this lifetime to accomplish.* It includes taking on various roles, experiencing pleasure, having meaningful relationships, being a catalyst, learning lessons, undergoing the death and rebirth processes, living authentically, discovering that you have free will, manifesting your dreams, and working through your life themes, etc. As this occurs you will come to *know your Truth* about your spirituality from your direct experience.

When you are living your 'being' (the totality of who you are), *you are living authentically*. This will make more sense as your human self comes into greater alignment with your soul.

You may grasp the Living in Alignment process intellectually, but *your direct experience* is the key to your transformation. You can become more inwardly focused and internally resourced to connect with your soul.

Your intention to access your soul is *the first step in becoming internally resourced.* Slowing down and becoming more present in your daily activities facilitates accessing your soul.

Your spirituality, or the act of living from your soul, is facilitated as soon as you begin *releasing yourself from the shackles of societal conditioning*, while at the same time learning to *become your own person*.

Exploring Your Spirituality

Living in Alignment is not affiliated with any religious organization, nor is it a *cult* (reflecting brainwashing and tribal consciousness). On the contrary, *you are intended to be your own leader.*

What if you are *your own best expert* when it comes to getting to know yourself and living your life? This is not to imply that you ignore or do not seek other people's advice, counsel, suggestions, guidance, or recommendations, for that would be nonsensical, could prove disastrous, and may possibly cause a lot of unnecessary hardship and suffering. After all, we do serve as catalysts for one another.

Living in Alignment will assist you to *become self-empowered* by listening to and following the guidance and prompting of your soul. At times your soul's prompting may be unconventional and may sound illogical to others. But remember that your soul has access to *'the bigger picture'* of your life, knows what is important for you to experience, and always has your best interests in the forefront. You are reminded to allow your soul to be *the final authority* in your life.

Your spirituality is also about acknowledging that *your life is of significance*, that you have your own life to live, and that you have your rightful place in the world. In this context *spirituality is about saying 'Yes!' to you and your life*.

A life worth living involves resourcing yourself from your soul instead of from your egoic mind.

Of course *you will be influenced* by other people, by your experiences, by societal dictates, by practical considerations, by your roles, and by all of your conditioning. It is always important to take these factors into account.

When you are able to get past the confines of your human mind and access the guidance and prompting of your soul, however, you will be able to open the door to *the life you are intended to live* fully and consciously.

The undercurrent of discontent you may feel (and manifest as mental, emotional, and physical conditions) can be the result of *missing out on the experiences you are intended to have* in your lifetime.

Developing Your Spiritual Practice

Developing your spiritual practice involves *discovering the needs of your soul* and going about meeting those needs. This requires living your life with your soul in the driver's seat.

A sustainable spiritual practice includes *quieting your mind* in order to access your soul's needs. Once you identify them, you then engage your human self and your mind to come up with realistic goals and manageable steps to meet those needs. In other words, *your soul informs your human self what its needs are and your human self takes care of the details*. This is the rightful role for your human self to perform.

As you identify and meet the needs of your soul, you will *experience meaning and purpose* in your life. Your spirituality is about *discovering and living up to your greatest potential*.

Another aspect of a spiritual practice involves *supporting, encouraging, and allowing* others to live up to their greatest potential.

When you are resourcing yourself from your soul, you will naturally want to live up to your full potential and invite others to do the same. You can truly serve others by reminding people at opportune times to tune into *who they are* and what they are *intended* to do in their lives.

Keep in mind that *no two spiritual practices look alike*. Your spiritual practice will be different from others'. This is understandable, because as a unique reflection of Source energy, each of us has a unique soul mission and thus different needs.

Your spiritual practices are also likely to *change as your awareness and needs change*. Be careful to avoid *rigidity* in your spiritual practices and also to avoid *imposing* your beliefs on others.

A healthy spiritual practice is *respectful* of other people's beliefs and practices, *unifies* people, and *deepens* your connection with Source energy and your own spirituality.

In addition, a healthy spiritual practice is about *living in balance* and *experiencing harmony,* which requires *identifying and meeting the needs of both your human self and your soul.*

Those who are *grounded* in their spirituality tend to *go within* to access the answers to their questions. It is about *trusting* that your answers are to be found within yourself rather than thinking that you need to be told by others what to believe and/or how to live your life.

Being grounded in your spirituality is also about *becoming your own authority* rather than living in *tribal consciousness* where following the leader is the norm. *Accessing your personal truth by distilling the insights, gifts, and lessons of your direct experiences* is the key to your authentic spirituality. Although you will take outside influences into account, you will allow your soul to be the *final authority* in your life.

Spirituality and Living in Alignment

When you acknowledge that you are as much a spiritual being as you are human, your *point of reference for living your life changes*.

Living in Alignment will offer you skills to move beyond viewing your life only from the three-dimensional reality you can see to include *multidimensional reality*. When this occurs your life will never be the same.

Instead of *believing* that Source energy exists, you will *come to know* that Source energy exists, based on your subjective experiences of Source energy working within your life.

GOD does not die on the day
when we cease to believe in a personal deity,
but we die on the day
when our lives cease to be illumined by
the steady radiance, renewed daily,
of a wonder,
the source of which is beyond all reason.

—Dag Hammarskjold

12

What Is Source Energy?

HAVING a relationship with Source energy may be difficult to grasp if you have been influenced by traditional religious beliefs or reacted against them. Living in Alignment is a process of modifying or changing beliefs that no longer support your recovery and tuning into *your experience of Source energy* in your life. Sustaining your recovery is about *consciously choosing* the relationship you have with Source energy and co-creating your transformed life.

Here are the main points explored in this chapter. I encourage you to entertain these concepts from the perspective of *'What if it is true?'* Check ☑ those that are most significant for your recovery or that you have questions or concerns about.

☐ Source energy and consciousness are synonymous.

☐ Source energy is a benevolent, intelligent, interactive, creative, ingenious, omnipresent, unifying, and self-regulating energy system.

☐ Source energy/consciousness is not static but is constantly evolving.

☐ Your understanding of Source energy will increase as your awareness increases.

☐ You can have a personal relationship with Source energy.

☐ Source energy is continuously offering you guidance; your task is to listen for this guidance and in turn utilize it.

☐ Source energy offers you guidance in many ways —including (but not limited to) your intuition, revelations and insights in your interactions with other people and all life forms, in your dreams, in mediation, etc.

☐ You always have the opportunity to discover your own truths about Source energy.

MY Forgiveness

I want to see what you see in me,
through your eyes windows of the soul.

I want to like what you like in me: my uniqueness.

I need to learn to love myself the way you love me.

Through my forgiveness I may begin to see
all that you see in me.

I began to see the greatest love I will ever know,
a power greater than myself, the God of my
understanding.

Through the eyes of my soul, the healing continues.

—Joanna Shaw

SOURCE energy is synonymous with **Conscious-ness itself**, which quantum physics has verified as being energy, the wellspring of life, what everybody and everything is made of. This energy cannot be created or destroyed. It can only be transformed! It is where our zest for living our lives originates. You can become increasingly aware of how you are **regulating** your energy and **co-creating** your reality.

Source energy is **a benevolent, intelligent, interactive, ingenious, creative, omnipresent, unifying, self-generating** energy system.

❖ **Benevolent:** Source energy is a loving presence in our lives.

❖ **Intelligent:** Source energy is the wellspring of universal wisdom.

❖ **Interactive:** you can interrelate with Source energy energetically as well as physically in your relationships with all life forms (because you and all life forms are unique reflections of Source energy).

❖ **Ingenious:** Source energy is highly skillful in its ability first to get the attention of, and then to work with your human self/egoic mind.

❖ **Creative:** Source energy is the life force energy inside you that you use to co-create.

❖ **Omnipresent:** Source energy is within all that is.

❖ **Unifying:** Source energy illuminates your interconnectedness with all life forms.

❖ *Self-generating energy system:* Source energy is continuously unfolding, creating, evolving, and transforming.

Your Unresolved Issues with Source Energy

Many people who have *disowned* their spirituality often deny, minimize, or are out of touch with how their *unresolved issues* with Source energy are affecting their lives. You may *have good reason to run away* from relating to Source energy. Here are some of the common ones. Check ☑ any that may apply to you:

☐ Those who experienced *early wounding* at the hands of their major caregivers (parents, educators, religious leaders) may transpose experiences of *neglect*, *indifference*, *abandonment*, and *betrayal* onto Source energy (or a higher Power) and thus want nothing to do with it.

☐ Those who grew up with no concept of a higher Power may consider themselves *atheists* (who don't believe in the existence of a deity) or

☐ *agnostics* (who claim neither faith in nor disbelief in God and who believe that nothing is known or can be known of the existence or nature of God or of anything beyond material phenomena).

☐ For varied reasons many people have limiting *beliefs*, *perceptions*, and *attitudes* about Source energy, along with

☐ unrealistic **understandings, expectations,** and **misconceptions.**

☐ In addition, some have **conflicting** thoughts about, are **angry** with, or hold **resentments** toward Source energy.

☐ Many live their lives attempting to **pull away from, sever,** or **disown** their connection with Source energy and thus **deny** their spirituality.

☐ For some, their disconnection from Source energy and their spirituality has resulted in living in *'victim consciousness'* or in **quiet desperation.**

☐ Others have totally identified with their human condition and are in complete **denial** of the existence (let alone the importance) of their **spiritual nature.** They rely totally on their **intellect** and are primarily **externally resourced.** Their belief system is embedded in **scientific reasoning:** the credo that if something can't be verified scientifically, it doesn't exist.

☐ Other people who feel **disconnected** from Source energy live **totally in their heads,** having only a peripheral connection with their physical bodies and **missing out** on the experience of being fully human.

☐ Some **want nothing to do with religion** and have mistakenly associated developing their connection with Source energy with **adopting religious beliefs.**

☐ Others give the impression they're **lost souls.**

Discover Your Soul Connection

There can be no *real* life (or no life worth living) without being conscious of your vital connection to Source energy.

Although our human minds will never be able to fully comprehend Source energy, you can become increasingly *aware* of the workings of Source energy in your life and in the lives of others. This increased awareness leads to increased understanding.

Living in Alignment taps into the core of all religious experience, which is the promise of a deepening connection with Source energy, one that *endures* any and all hardship, condition, circumstance, and the like. Living in Alignment is *inclusive* of all religious experiences that aim to foster *unity consciousness*.

Living in Alignment will assist you to move out of *tribal consciousness* (where following a leader is the norm) and experience a direct and *personal connection* with Source energy via your relationship with your soul.

YOU cannot expect
the world to change
until you change yourself.
—Robert Muller

Your Relationship with Source Energy

You get to decide *what kind of relationship you want with Source energy*. How much conscious awareness of Source energy (within yourself, others, and all life forms) do you want to have?

Living in Alignment fosters an *interdependent relationship* with Source energy as an alternative to either *disowning* your spirituality or *depending* on religious leaders to administer to your spiritual needs.

Your soul *needs* your human self to be its hands and feet (or its agent), while your human self *needs* your soul to gain access to 'the bigger picture' of your life.

Source Energy is Continuing to Evolve

What if it is true that *all* your circumstances, conditions, events, issues, problems, and concerns are *benefiting* you? And what if it is true that Source energy is *evolving* through each of us via the experiences life offers us? While embracing *all* of your life experiences, you can become increasingly conscious of their *significance* and the workings of Source energy in your life.

Your soul is a unique manifestation of Source energy. It *lives* simultaneously in both the seen and the unseen worlds. It comes into any particular incarnation with a particular soul mission. *It does not die* with the death of your physical body.

Your soul has direct access to the particulars of your life, including *why* you're here and *what* you're here to accomplish within any given lifetime.

Guidance is Being Continuously Offered

Source energy is continuously offering you *guidance* in all aspects of your life, such as

❖ your relationship with *your human self*

❖ your *career* and avocation

❖ your *interactions* with others

❖ *the next step* to take in your life

❖ wake-up calls when you're off track in terms of your *soul mission* (life calling)

❖ wake-up calls when you're not *living in balance*

You have only to receive this guidance, follow the prompting from your soul, and in turn *integrate* the insights, gifts, and lessons being offered in the context of your experiences.

As you develop your awareness, you will come to understand the particulars of how Source energy works in your life, and even more importantly, how Source energy is always available to facilitate living up to your full potential.

If you hear your soul's guidance but choose not to utilize it, you are truly missing out on the experiences that you are intended to have in your life. This is why developing your awareness is so important. It is facilitated by becoming fully present in your daily living. Keep in mind that Source energy is offering you guidance in numerous ways. Pay attention to and examine your *body sensations, promptings, insights, synchronicities, hunches, revelations, and dreams*.

About Your Prayers and Invocations

You may have prayed to Source energy but do not always receive answers. When this occurs, you may not be paying close enough attention to how guidance is being offered, or perhaps *your expectations* about how that guidance *should* be offered are preventing you from receiving it.

Your human self/egoic mind may prefer *not to know the answers* to the questions you are posing to Source energy or the *truth* about some aspect of your life. Or you may realize that the guidance being offered will entail *making changes* that you are afraid of making, or you do not want to *take full responsibility* for your life. In working with Source energy, a rule of thumb is that if you don't want to know the truth about something, *don't ask*.

Be careful *not* to allow your mind to convince you that Source energy is *nowhere to be found* in your life, because this is simply not the case. You will deepen your experience of Source energy as you become more internally resourced. Although you may never be able to fully comprehend the workings of Source energy, opportunities to experience its magnificence directly are always offered in your life.

THE Road Not Taken

Two roads diverged in a yellow wood,
And sorry I could not travel both
And be one traveler, long I stood
And looked down one as far as I could
To where it bent in the undergrowth;

Then took the other, as just as fair,
And having perhaps the better claim,
Because it was grassy and wanted wear;
Though as for that the passing there
Had worn them really about the same,

And both that morning equally lay
In leaves no step had trodden black.
Oh, I kept the first for another day!
Yet knowing how way leads on to way,
I doubted if I should ever come back.

I shall be telling this with a sigh
Somewhere ages and ages hence:
Two roads diverged in a wood, and I —
I took the one less traveled by,
And that has made all the difference.

—Robert Frost

13

Becoming Internally Resourced

BECOMING internally resourced is a *choice* you make. It's your option to decide whether or not you want to *deepen* your connection with Source energy, *how much* you want to deepen your awareness, and *how conscious* of this connection you want to be.

Developing your capacity to be Living in Alignment is *simple* both in theory and in practice.

Believe it or not, everyone on Planet Earth is already Living in Alignment to a lesser or greater extent, whether or not you are aware of this reality. Many people are in the dark about their capacity to *accelerate* their process of personal transformation and become increasingly conscious of the *benefits* of Living in Alignment in their daily lives.

Your subjective experiences of Living in Alignment will offer your mind the *proof* it needs to feel confident that Living in Alignment is a *practical*, *effective*, and *trustworthy* approach to living your life, and one that will yield remarkable results.

Your subjective experiences will also reveal that your soul is more *capable*, more *qualified*, more *experienced*, and more *skilled* at being in the driver's seat and leading your life than the alternative of relying primarily on the resources of your intellect/mind. Your societal conditioning is *limited* by the dominant cultural biases, beliefs, attitudes, values, mores, perspectives, and the like.

You will strive to be *more conscious* of becoming internally resourced as your mind realizes that this yields *favorable* results — such as

❖ having greater *success* in your life

❖ feeling *confident*

❖ generating high *self-esteem*

❖ experiencing more energy and *power*

❖ becoming proficient at *manifesting* your dreams

❖ realizing your *life calling*

❖ developing *satisfying*/nourishing relationships

❖ feeling *safe and secure* in your body

❖ discovering more enjoyment, passion, balance, happiness, connection, and *freedom to be* yourself.

When you attend to *your intuition* (what feels 'right') and learn to listen to and follow the guidance and prompting of your soul, you will become more internally resourced.

Like many who lack a healthy connection to their soul, you may be convinced that *you are* your ego-centered mind. You think that you are *only* your human self, that Source energy doesn't exist, that you are *alone* in the Universe, and that life has *no meaning* and purpose.

This is the result of being identified primarily with your humanness and being externally re-sourced. This state of being is called *'mistaken identity'*. A lack of a healthy connection with your soul can lead to mental, emotional, physical, and spiritual *'dis-ease'* and conditions.

Becoming internally resourced is a lifelong prac-tice of *deepening* your connection with Source energy while becoming increasingly aware of the *wondrous unfolding* of your life. Living in Align-ment is your *birthright*, a naturally occurring pro-cess that is unique to every person.

Your soul witnesses your human self going about completing your soul mission, and when you're *off track* or heading in that direction, when you need a *breakthrough*, or when certain tasks are coming to completion, your soul will get the attention of your human self by issuing *wake-up calls* that become more pronounced if *ignored* or not followed.

You have *free will* regarding the *kind* of relation-ship you want to have with your soul, and can *de-cide* whether or not you want that relationship to be *conscious*.

Becoming internally resourced is much more than having an intellectual understanding of a concept. It is *an alternative way of being and living your life*. It involves changing your orientation *from* being identified primarily with your human self and the *conditioning* of the three-dimensional world *to* having a **conscious connection** with your soul and **allowing** your soul to lead your life.

There is a **qualitative difference** between being externally resourced and being internally resourced. The Living in Alignment process will illuminate this difference and assist you to experience it.

Learning to trust the guidance from your soul is less about **figuring out** your life and more about **feeling your way** into it. It's not that you stop using your mind or discard logical, rational, linear ways of thinking, but rather that you **apply** these important skills in service of your soul's directives.

You have the option of **allowing** your soul to lead your life. The existential answers you seek about the particulars of your life are to be found in the depths of your soul, **not** within the confines of societal conditioning/dictates. Your life has a unique **flow**, and you can learn to **trust** and live fully in that flow.

Following your soul's directives (versus your mind) is the most **desirable, advantageous,** and **gratifying** way to live your life. The more your mind allows your soul to be in the proverbial driver's seat, the more you will become aware of the wonders of its workings in your life as you gain an increasing assurance of the '**rightness**' of living in partnership with your soul.

The more you are internally resourced, the more you will become **self-empowered** and move into a position of becoming your own authority.

Your soul will provide opportunities to place you where you need to be, meeting the people you need to meet, and doing what you need to be doing in each chapter of your life.

Some of the workings of your soul manifest in all aspects of living your life: synchronicities, dreams, premonitions, revelations, realizations, music, movies, books, through other people, the Ah-ha's, ideas, gut responses. Anything and anybody can serve as a means by which your soul communicates with you.

As you become internally resourced by deferring to your soul for guidance and following that guidance, a *profound awakening* will occur. The experience of *soul realization* (recognizing that you have a soul) leads to *soul actualization* (living up to your full potential and realizing your soul mission), which culminates in experiencing *soul fulfillment*.

S ORROW prepares you for joy.
It violently sweeps everything
out of your house, so that
new joy can find space to enter.
It shakes the yellow leaves
from the bough of your heart, so that
fresh, green leaves can grow in their place.
It pulls up the rotten roots, so that
new roots hidden beneath have room to grow.
Whatever sorrow shakes from your heart,
far better things will take their place.

—Jalāl al-Dīn Rūmī

I WENT from loving strife
to loving life
from seeing only violence and pain
to seeing the potential in every gain.

People spend their time
worrying and arguing over
the smallest of things

When they should obsess
and fight for the smallest
of wings.

Rites of passage
taken to addicts
helping us to find a balance.

The days you are weak
make you stronger,
so pray they last a little longer.

I am who I am
I can and I can't
the daily battle inside rages.

The key to life,
locked beneath pain and strife,
is the key to seeing differently.

—Jeff Arena

14

Why is it so difficult to access my soul?

IT is your human self, and more specifically your *conditioning*, that prevents you from accessing your soul. Living in Alignment will assist you to experience your soul's presence in your life and learn how to *partner* with your soul (Source energy within). Living in Alignment will also help you become increasingly more conscious/*aware* of the presence of your soul in your life.

By conditioning I refer to how your beliefs, thought forms, attitudes, perceptions, expectations, feelings, behaviors, and intentions are influencing your *connection* with your soul (or lack thereof).

Believe it or not, you alone are *choosing* the type of relationship you're having with your soul from moment to moment. You may be totally *unaware* of this experience. As in all relationships, it is your responsibility to nurture your connection with your soul. Whatever you put into *deepening* your relationship with your soul will be reflected in the quality of your connection.

Living in a *fear-based reality* hinders or outright prevents nurturing your soul connection, for when you live in fear, your energy level is lowered and your human self goes into sympathetic (fight or flight) mode. Living in fear is an indicator of being primarily externally resourced (**stuck** in your head), making it difficult to access your intuition or hear the **voice** of your soul. The more externally focused you are (identified with your human self and the three-dimensional world) the more you tend to live in fear.

Fear plays out as your human self (or your mind) wanting a guarantee, needing instant gratification, having resistance, doubts, and confusion, attempting to control the outcome, futurizing, etc.

It is also important to develop your ability to move from a **literal** understanding of events, circumstances, and experiences of your life to discover their **symbolic** meaning.

Like the air you breathe, your soul is always present. You have only to open up to 'the bigger picture' of how all of the experiences you're having in life are benefiting you and are integral to accomplishing your **soul mission** or calling in life.

Your intellect **gets in the way** of deepening your connection with your soul by being impatient, jumping to conclusions, making hasty assumptions, aborting a process (a form of abandoning yourself), fearing the unknown, second-guessing, confusion, doubt, apprehension, being attached to a particular outcome, comparing your life to other peoples' lives, having a limiting view of Trust and Surrender ('giving up' vs. a merging of energy), and/or wanting instant gratification.

Everything that has happened, is happening, or will happen to you has the *inherent potential* of benefiting you. In other words all of your experiences are *intended* to provide you with maximum benefit. Your task is to train your mind to identify the insights, gifts, and lessons being offered and to *integrate* these into your behaviors.

Trust and *Surrender* are two of the most important requirements for your egoic mind to grasp and develop. Without this skill set in place, it becomes very difficult for your mind to listen to and follow the guidance of your soul.

The more your human self is identified with the three-dimensional world, the more difficult it may be to Trust and Surrender. Instead you will rely on your egoic mind that wants to stay in the driver's seat and will tend to *control* the outcome. To Trust and Surrender, your ego must *relinquish the illusion* that you can control the creative flow of Source energy that pulsates within you and all life forms.

Trust and Surrender are about changing your *point of reference*, allowing your mind to defer to your soul for guidance. When truly integrated into your life, Trust and Surrender are intended to *transform* your way of being and living in the world.

Your ability to Trust and Surrender directly impacts the *type* of relationship you have with your soul and the world of Mystery. While having an open mind and heart are necessary to access your soul, Trust and Surrender are essential to *deepening* your connection with your soul.

The act of trusting in and surrendering to your soul is always *advantageous* — with no exceptions. You will be able to test this out for yourself.

The *interplay* of opening your mind and your heart fosters the development of your *intuition*, which is the voice of your soul.

You are *intended* to go about living your life in partnership with your soul. By listening to and following your soul's *guidance* you develop a *partnership* with your soul. This is a cooperative venture in which your human self becomes the *agent* of your soul.

In contrast, when you are primarily externally resourced you are living in fear, resulting in *worrying*. Worrying lowers your energy level by demanding a lot of energy. Worrying is an indicator that you are *not trusting* in Source energy and not working in partnership with your soul.

Your need to *control and manipulate* are indicators that your *ego* is getting in your way. Contrary to popular misconceptions, trusting in your soul is *not* about having blind faith, and surrendering is *not* about becoming powerless. Trust involves *yielding* to your soul, and Surrender involves *merging* with your soul. Practicing Trust and Surrender translates to listening to and following the *guidance* from your soul.

15

Resolving Power and Authority Issues

CLAIMING your personal power and Living in Alignment with your internal authority (your soul) is challenging for anyone emerging from the struggle and confusion of surrendering authority and power to dependence. Many in recovery have either been abused or abusers, feel disempowered, distrust external authority figures, fear misusing their power, or have issues with the concept of a higher Power. *Sustaining your recovery* is about experiencing your power and living out your wholeness, your full potential, and your unique calling.

Here are the main points explored in this chapter. I encourage you to entertain these concepts from the perspective of *'What if it is true?'* Check ☑ those that are most significant for your recovery or that you have questions or concerns about.

☐ You can develop the skills to become your own best expert and authority.

☐ Living authentically is synonymous with staying in your power.

☐ If you don't claim your power, someone or something else will.

☐ When you give your power away, you live in 'victim consciousness'.

- ☐ Establishing and maintaining healthy boundaries helps you stay empowered.

- ☐ Saying a resounding *'Yes!'* to yourself and your life keeps you in your power.

- ☐ No one or no thing can have authority over you unless you give it to them.

- ☐ Reclaiming your energy is self-empowering.

- ☐ Owning all aspects of your reality (mental, emotional, physical, and spiritual) is self-empowering.

- ☐ Accessing and meeting your human and soul needs keeps you self-empowered.

MT Everest

In my dream my mountain stands before me
Again and again

I see my worn footsteps
The tragic attempts of my past

You see I had become the failed mountaineer
Only to return again and again

Now I see new footsteps in the present
and see the woman I was always meant to be

As I gaze upon my beautiful, beautiful mountain
of hope, the tears fall from my face
again and again, full of joy and wonder

—Joanna Shaw

POWER and authority are important topics, for they are integral components of the Living in Alignment process. You may discover that you have unresolved issues with one or both. When you have not examined your relationship to these issues, it is likely that your limiting thought patterns are getting in the way of living up to your full potential.

Your power comes from Source energy. We are all made of the same energy. When you are connected to that energy, you experience self-empowerment.

Self-empowerment is the result of your human self coming into alignment with your soul. It is the qualitative experience of being *soul-realized.* The more you become soul-realized, the more you are self-empowered.

Your self-empowerment offers you *increasing amounts of energy.* It is the creative force of the Universe. To achieve your greatest potential, you can learn to train your mind and physical body to *regulate* your energy.

You may have a limiting view of power because of what you have been taught or conditioned to believe about it. For example, you may have the mistaken belief that *power is inherently bad.* Consequently you may be afraid of power, either your own or that of others. You may also correlate power with its *abuse.* Understandably so: the abuse of power and authority is found in every sector of society. *Everyone has witnessed some sort of abuse of power* in their own lives as well as in the lives of others.

Abusing Your Power

Abuse of power takes many forms: psychological, emotional, spiritual, physical, and sexual. It can be hidden or blatant. Similarly, you may equate power with *force*. Power equates to Source energy, while *force is the use of energy to attempt to control and manipulate people.*

When you are primarily externally resourced, you are likely to abuse your power. You may be motivated by greed, power, or lust, as well as by your insecurities (such as low self-esteem). When you are primarily externally resourced, you are also likely to be out of touch with the underlying needs of your soul.

Indeed, many people who are mostly externally resourced do not acknowledge that they even have a soul. In addition, when you are externally resourced, you live in a fear-based reality and are primarily focused on your survival needs.

Furthermore, when you are externally resourced you do not have access to the universal truth that we are all interconnected and interdependent. *This lack of awareness fosters egocentrism*, which leads to the abuse of your power.

Your Power *Is* Energy

To reiterate, your power **is** energy! *Your intentions, along with how you are resourced, (internally or externally) will determine how you use your power.* The more you become aware of your core self (your soul), the more energy you will generate. This is the energy you use to co-create your reality.

You may not be aware that when you become soul-realized you have tapped into Source energy. Your soul is a unique reflection of Source energy. Call this energy whatever you are most comfortable with: the God within, Consciousness itself, Divine energy. It doesn't matter as long as you know that you are referring to it as the life-giving Source.

Another reason why you may not want to 'own' your power is because *being in your power requires being responsible for yourself and your life.* For various reasons (such as inertia, immaturity, low self-esteem, 'victim consciousness'), you may not want to take ownership of your power or become self-empowered. Instead, you just give it away.

You may not understand how to manage your energy (power) effectively. In addition, you may consciously or subconsciously *fear* that you will *abuse your power* or position of authority. This is a valid concern, especially when you are mostly externally resourced.

You may have been taught that you entered this life as a sinner, and that your life **should** be focused on repenting for your sins. This type of conditioning is a sure way to subdue your personal power.

Many religious organizations try to convince you that you are incapable of managing your own life, and that someone else has to take over. Organized religions have often perpetuated a **tribal mentality** (suppressing your individual identity), fostered **infantilism** (taking care of you and telling you what to believe), and encouraged **codependence** (being dependent upon others to feel whole).

Thus **many people see religious dogma as a form of control and manipulation**. The legacy of unexamined religious belief may lead you to live a life of quiet desperation, immersed in fear, shame, and guilt, and susceptible to yielding your power to misguided religious and spiritual leaders.

Source Energy and Your Personal History

If your childhood relationship with your parents was **less than nurturing** (if you were neglected, betrayed, or abandoned), your experience will likely get transferred to your relationship with Source energy.

If as a child your relationship with your parents was **estranged**, you may also have an estranged relationship with Source energy. This is why you may have difficulty with the concept of a higher Power, let alone the idea of being in relationship with it. *You may simply react to the concept itself because you haven't examined your beliefs.*

In addition, you may have experienced *spiritual abuse* at some point in your life. Until these issues get resolved, you are likely to confuse your higher Power with your parents or religious leaders, feeling that Source energy has somehow betrayed or abandoned you. Understandably, you may have inadvertently left a higher Power out of the equation, *abandoning Source energy within yourself.* Is it any wonder you may feel an emptiness inside?

Living in Alignment is not about *handing over* your power to your soul (Source energy within), but rather *a merging of your human self with your soul so that the two are working in partnership and your human self becomes the agent of your soul.*

You may have an estranged relationship with Source energy because subconsciously you think that Source energy doesn't have your best interests in the forefront. Understandably, you may have erroneously concluded that Source energy is a *menacing, antagonistic, and punishing force* that doesn't want you to experience pleasure, happiness, passion, bliss, or fulfillment. Consequently you may fear Source energy and want as little to do with it as possible.

Source energy is *not a person* but Consciousness itself: an omnipresent energy source that is benevolent, interactive, ingenious, creative, and unifying. Moreover, it is an energy you can partner with, one that always keeps your best interests in the fore-front.

If you decide that traditional religious teachings have **distorted** your experience and understanding of Source energy, you can reclaim your spiritual power by **choosing** concepts that expand your mind and open your heart.

Your Relationship with Power

You may have used power to control and manipulate others, or have been on the receiving end of its abuse. As a result you may shy away from consciously embracing it. Yet **your power is energy**, and we are all made up of energy. What you **do** with your energy or power is the question.

❖ What is your **relationship** to power?

❖ Will you use it to help make this world a **better** place for everyone?

❖ Or will your mind use it only to focus on your own **needs** and wants?

❖ Will you allow other people to **abuse** you with their power?

These are important issues to consider. Living in Alignment will assist you to access more and more of your energy or power. Simply stated, **the more connected you are to your soul, the more power you will have at your disposal**.

You have the daily opportunity to experience your relationship with power and authority. **We** *serve as mirrors for one another.* Chances are that what you don't like in other people playing out their power is what you don't like or can't accept in yourself, or *fear* of what would happen if you actually *'own'* your power.

You may not respect people in authority because you've had direct experiences of their *abuse* of power. If you do not work it through, this gets carried over into your life. For example, if you have unresolved power issues you may experience difficulty being in a position of power, or may not even allow yourself to be in that type of position.

Looking in the Mirror

Coming home to yourself by experiencing Source energy both in yourself and in the world around you results in vitality, enjoyment, awareness, passion, wisdom, courage, connection, contentment, happiness, balance, and fulfillment. This will not occur, however, if consciously or unconsciously you do not want to experience Source energy in your life.

No wonder you may experience so much internal conflict. You may spend a lot of time attempting to run away from yourself and from your higher Power within. Living in Alignment will *help you look yourself in the mirror and reconnect with your essence: your soul.*

If you are resourcing yourself from your societal conditioning, you are limiting yourself to an external authority. Being in a position of authority is about holding energy or power. *If you are unwilling or unable to hold your own power, it will be easy for outside influences to have power over you.* You have to *claim* your power, which is the same as claiming the Source energy within you. This is reaffirmed by your ways of thinking, your choices and decisions, and every action you take.

Who or what has authority over you? Is it your work? Money? Status? The good news is that you get to decide *how* you experience your own power and authority. *You are always co-creating your reality* in every moment.

When you are in Living in Alignment, you can be certain that *your soul will do everything possible to prevent you from abusing your power.* Your soul, in its wisdom, will illuminate any issues you have with power and authority and prompt you to discern how to go about dealing with and resolving those issues. This is not a guarantee, however, because you will tend to *abuse* your power or position of authority when your human self is not Living in Alignment or working in partnership with your soul.

Becoming Your Own Authority

The Living in Alignment process is intended to help you go within and access your truth, which in turn teaches you to become your own authority. *You are your own best expert* when it comes to living up to your full potential. *The more you are aligned with your soul, the more energy you can access and have available to you.* Living in Alignment will help you learn how to regulate this energy and channel it to accomplish your calling in life.

What do you do with your power and authority? Learning to take responsibility for this energy is of utmost importance. It is essential to living in balance and harmony. *The 'right' relationship to your power and authority may be different for you*, however, than for others.

When in a position of authority, it is crucial to keep in the forefront the *welfare and wellbeing* of everyone, including all life forms and the Planet itself.

❖ If your soul mission involves being in a leadership position, will you lead from your *soul?*

❖ Will you *promote* unity consciousness?

❖ Or will you lead from *fear?*

❖ How do you intend to *use* your power?

These are important questions to answer.

If you don't 'own' your power, something (like an addiction) *or someone else will.* This is the number one reason why you need to become your own authority, embodying your power while assisting others to do the same. You can learn to *have authority* over your human self. In part this is about *taking responsibility* for your life and holding yourself accountable. This is how you maintain and deepen in your power.

In addition, it is imperative to **establish and maintain healthy boundaries with yourself and others** if you are to live an empowered life. Living in Alignment will help you understand the different types of boundaries and develop the skill base to utilize those boundaries effectively.

Living Up to Your Full Potential

As you clarify your relationship with power and authority, you will also learn about working with energy. Living in Alignment is about **reclaiming your power from those to whom you have given it away or from debilitating behaviors** such as dependence. This practice is self-empowering, energizing, and is intended for the purpose of living up to your full potential.

As you become more internally resourced, you will come to know that your life has meaning and purpose: that you have a **calling** in your life. As your human self partners with your soul, you will gain access both to 'the bigger picture' view of your life and the details of that calling. You will come to realize the importance of learning effective ways to partner with energy and become your own authority.

This does not exclude listening to or being influenced by others, seeking their counsel and advice, or supporting those in positions of authority. **Being your own authority means that when all is said and done, you are the final author of your life.** This means

❖ holding yourself *accountable* and taking responsibility

❖ doing the *right* thing for yourself in order to stay empowered

❖ always being mindful of the welfare of *other* people and species

❖ *choosing* to experience more enjoyment, vitality, power, passion, satisfaction, and contentment

❖ not being controlled or manipulated by societal *dictates*

❖ speaking out against or doing what you can about the *injustices* happening around you whenever possible.

You alone must claim your power; no one else can do this for you. It is also your choice as to how you want to live your life. Until you claim your life, it is likely that you will continue to live in 'victim consciousness' to a greater or lesser degree. This is because other people, organizations, behaviors, and societal pressures will assume authority over you if you do not claim your power.

Saying a resounding 'Yes!' *to yourself and your life* will enable you to reclaim your power and authority. You will discover that *you are not alone*, and that you are being guided by your soul every step of the way. This guidance will present itself in many forms: dreams, people, inclinations, synchronicities, body sensations, visualizations, revelations, ideas, hunches, books, music, art, etc.

OUR Deepest Fear

Our deepest fear is
not that we are inadequate.

Our deepest fear is
that we are powerful beyond measure.

It is our light, not our darkness,
that most frightens us.

We ask ourselves,
Who am I to be brilliant,
gorgeous, talented, fabulous?

Actually, who are you not to be?
You are a child of God.

Your playing small
does not serve the world.

There is nothing enlightened
about shrinking so that
other people won't feel insecure around you.

We are all meant to shine,
as children do.

We were born to make manifest
the glory of God
that is within us.

It's not just in some of us;
it is in everyone.

And as we let our own light shine,
we unconsciously give other people
permission to do the same.

As we are liberated
from our own fear,
our presence
automatically liberates others.

—Marianne Williamson

16

Examining Your Beliefs and Thinking

RECOVERING your power from the experience of *dependence* on a substance or a behavior begins with facing your beliefs and other thought patterns that have supported your addiction. This is about *discovering and telling your own truth* and letting go of ways of thinking that do not serve your wholeness and *freedom to be*. Your *judgments, perceptions, emotions,* and *body sensations* will bring you face to face with your beliefs. You get to decide which of these you want to keep, modify, or change altogether.

Here are the main points explored in this chapter. Consider these as *working hypotheses*. Open your mind to the possibility that they are *effective and reliable*. Experience for yourself what happens when you consider these concepts from the perspective of *'What if it is true?'* Allow yourself to have a *direct experience* of these concepts in your day-to-day living. Check ☑ those that are most significant for your recovery or that you have questions or concerns about.

☐ By closely examining your beliefs and ways of thinking, you can discern how they are impacting every aspect of your life.

☐ Beliefs and ways of thinking are like lenses and filters that affect how you see the world and experience the circumstances in your life.

☐ Your beliefs and ways of thinking can be modified or changed.

☐ Whatever you say *'I am'* to has a way of claiming your power and your life.

☐ All the events, circumstances, experiences, conditions, issues, and problems in your life have the 'inherent potential' of benefiting you.

☐ 'Victim consciousness' is the result of your inability or unwillingness to view yourself and your life from a broader perspective: you are a co-creator of your reality.

☐ As your awareness increases, so too will your understanding, which in turn impacts your beliefs and ways of thinking.

☐ Your beliefs create powerful fields of energy, helping to keep you imprisoned in the past or serving as a springboard to take you into the future. Your beliefs can be either empowering or disempowering as a result.

☐ Your beliefs and ways of thinking have a direct impact on your emotional reality, which in turn has a direct impact on your behaviors.

PRACTICE is the hardest part of learning, and training is the essence of transformation.
—Ann Voskamp

BELIEFS are the fabric of your life. Whether or not you are conscious of them, beliefs and other thought patterns become *the underpinnings of your thinking*.

Your mind/intellect is the sum total of your conditioning: your beliefs, thought forms, attitudes, perceptions, expectations, assumptions, judgments, and interpretations.

The good news is that *beliefs and ways of thinking can be modified or changed* altogether. You can also develop new beliefs and ways of thinking to replace those you have discarded.

You can examine your beliefs and ways of thinking and determine for yourself how some may be limiting you, not benefiting you, or getting in the way of your recovery and your life.

Until you do that, *you will remain in the dark and be unable to understand their impact on all aspects of your life:* in relationships, living up to your full potential, living authentically, finding meaning and purpose in your life, co-creating your reality, and experiencing satisfaction and fulfillment.

Beliefs are thoughts that become set energy patterns when repeated over and over again. In your everyday life, *beliefs function like lenses* that promote seeing life from a particular point of view.

If, for example, you believe you cannot live your life without your drug of choice, your mind will find proof of this. Indeed, it will actually filter out all

151

information that could challenge or disprove this notion and find only supporting evidence to validate your belief. Thus you are *trapped in your beliefs* about your addiction.

Adopting Other People's Beliefs and Thinking

You may be surprised to discover that what you consider to be *your* beliefs are in actuality *the beliefs of others that you have adopted.*

The beliefs you share with others form the common bonds that develop into friendships, support groups, organizations, marriages, and business partnerships. Beliefs divide people as well, leading to discrimination, marginalization, divisiveness, and in extreme cases, war.

Your mind receives information like a sponge. *You are easily susceptible to societal conditioning* before you develop the capacity to think for yourself. This is why your so-called 'formative' years, especially from infancy through early childhood, have so much impact on your character development.

People who share the same beliefs create *an energy field* that can be quite powerful. This energy has the potential to be highly influential, and depending on how it is channeled, can be used *to unify* as easily as *to divide*.

You will want to be discerning about the people with whom you associate as well as the organizations with which you affiliate. *If you do not have healthy boundaries*, you will tend to take on the beliefs of those particular people and organizations. This includes all social systems—familial, religious, educational, political, corporate, etc.

Your *family of origin* has a particularly powerful influence on your life. Becoming your authentic self is greatly impacted by your early conditioning, including:

❖ your earliest contact, when you were the most *susceptible* to conditioning

❖ the *dependence* you have on your primary caregivers to provide for your basic needs

❖ the close *proximity* to and duration of time spent with your family.

Developing your processing skills will help ensure that your beliefs and ways of thinking are *truly your own* and not those that have been *imposed* on you by other people or institutions.

Your Socialization Is Indoctrination

Your socialization process can be viewed as a form of *indoctrination*. Our public education system prepares you to *assimilate into the dominant culture*.

The media are a pervasive influence *perpetuating conformity*. Indoctrination has become *an unconscious process* for many people.

The Power of Your Beliefs

What you say 'I am' to has a way of claiming your life. Before a belief becomes a belief, it is a message or thought form. As you focus on it by repeating it over and over again, it develops into an energetic pattern.

Beliefs create powerful currents of energy. They can become *a springboard* to your freedom as easily as they can keep you *chained* to what you don't want.

When you state that *'I am an alcoholic'* you are, in effect, *identifying with your condition*, rather than saying 'I am in recovery from addiction.' When you *over-identify with* or *internalize* your conditions, you proclaim that *you are* your conditions.

What You Know vs. What You Believe

What you believe and what you know are not necessarily one and the same. Knowing is the result of *having experienced* something directly, while believing something is not necessarily based on your subjective experience. Your beliefs can be based on a purely *intellectual understanding* that is logical, linear, and rational. In other words it makes sense to you.

You may also have beliefs that you do not actually agree with because something was *instilled* in your mind at an early age. Some of your beliefs may have always been there or may have become so pervasive that you are *unconscious* of them. *Your beliefs and ways of thinking directly impact your emotions as well as your behaviors.*

Your unexamined beliefs and ways of thinking will *always* have an impact on all aspects of your life. You can both believe in something and at the same time have knowledge of it. You can *believe* that Source energy exists, and also *know* this is true based on your subjective experiences of Source energy working in your life.

Your Beliefs and Interpretations

Your beliefs develop from how *your mind interprets the events, circumstances, and conditions* that surround you. Your experience is affected by many variables, including your current beliefs, that function as *both lenses and filters.*

Your beliefs directly impact your perceptions, while your perceptions reinforce your beliefs. Your limiting beliefs do *not* facilitate your best interests and will *perpetuate what you don't want.*

This is why it is so important both to identify and to examine your beliefs and ways of thinking: they hold the key to *understanding and changing the reality* you are constantly co-creating.

Your mind can be a *loyal servant* or a *terrible tyrant.* Do not treat your mind as *the enemy* or something to be annihilated. Your soul needs your mind (and your human self) to *accomplish your mission* in life.

You are deprogramming and reprogramming your mind, not your soul. **_You decide_** which beliefs and ways of thinking you want to change or replace. This leads to living authentically and finding meaning and purpose in your life.

When Your Beliefs and Thinking Are in the Way

When your human self is in the driver's seat, your overall sense of wellbeing **_becomes jeopardized_** because you are not living in the truth of who you are.

When you are **_internally resourced_** you are **_in relationship_** with both your soul and your human self. In establishing this partnership **_your human self merges with your soul_**, which then helps ensure that the needs of both get met.

Your soul will inform your human self when your **_limiting beliefs and thinking patterns_** are getting in the way. From this list of signs that you are '_off track,_' check ☑ those you experience:

☐ feeling **_stuck_**

☐ repeating unwanted **_dysfunctional_** behavioral patterns such as addictions and self-deprecation

☐ **_judging_** yourself and/or others

☐ **_comparing_** yourself to other people or relating to them from a one-up or one-down position

☐ feeling out of balance, over-extended, resentful, or on the verge of **_burnout_**

☐ experiencing unhappiness or **_angst_**

☐ feeling *disconnected* from yourself and your relationships

☐ not knowing what your *needs* are

☐ exhibiting *poor* health

☐ being *inauthentic*

☐ feeling that your heart is *closed*

☐ knowing somehow that your life has taken a *wrong* turn

☐ feeling *unfulfilled*

☐ *reacting* versus responding to what is happening in your life

☐ being highly *defended*

☐ feeling *anxiety*-ridden

☐ attempting to *control* others

☐ experiencing a *lack* of spontaneity

☐ being *cynical.*

These are indications that *your beliefs and ways of thinking are sabotaging your life.* This is your cue to *look inward* to identify and examine how your human self is getting in your way.

Beliefs and thinking patterns do *not* get modified or changed *on their own.* It will take *a conscious effort* on your part. This does not require endless processing, but it will demand discipline, determination, attentiveness, and courage.

Skills to Work with Your Beliefs and Thinking

Living in Alignment provides *life skills* that are vital to *deprogramming* and *reprogramming* your beliefs and thinking patterns. These include:

- ❖ re-parenting *yourself*
- ❖ becoming *your* own best friend
- ❖ challenging your *limiting* beliefs
- ❖ 'letting go and letting *God*'
- ❖ developing an attitude of *gratitude*
- ❖ recognizing that you always have *choices*
- ❖ becoming *solution*-oriented
- ❖ *reframing* your thoughts
- ❖ being *fully* aware of each day's opportunities
- ❖ developing your *mindfulness* skills
- ❖ working with your *energy* field.

Focusing on and clarifying your intentions is one of the most effective ways to direct your mind like a laser beam, creating a powerful energy field.

Your intentions help your human self bypass the trappings of your limiting beliefs and thinking patterns in order to access directly what is most important. Your intentions will help your human self get out of the drama of your 'story' by expanding your consciousness: looking for the opportunities in your life, examining all your options, and tuning into 'what wants to happen' or *what you're longing to experience*. Focusing on your intentions helps keep you *empowered*.

Knowing Your Whole Truth

With increased awareness comes increased understanding. As this occurs, your human self will want your beliefs and ways of thinking to be as congruent as possible with *the whole truth of who you are*. When *shifts* (permanent changes) take place in your internal reality (energetically, mentally, emotionally, physically, and behaviorally), they will be reflected in all aspects of your external reality.

Living in Alignment is intended to assist you to access *your truth* concerning every aspect of your life and help you develop a *skill base* so that you can *live in your truth*.

Living in Alignment is *the life-long journey of deepening in relationship to your human self and your soul*, which in turn facilitates deepening in all your relationships, including the one you have with life itself. You will become more conscious of this process as well as encouraged to experience its benefits each step of the way.

Living in Alignment will affirm, inspire, excite, and motivate you to experience that *your relationship with your soul and the world of mystery is just as real as your relationship with your external world*. An incredible journey awaits you, one of awakening to the magnificence of who you are while appreciating the wonders that surround you.

LIFE'S Terms

I've tried so hard
unsure it was worth it
I've changed so much
feel more imperfect

Expected much better
nothing like this
The things I touch
still turn to shit

Look at my family
I know what they're thinking
They miss the old me
the me that was using

The me that seemed strong
that I was abusing
The me that was funny
whose thoughts weren't amusing

Look in my mind
see something disturbing:
That me was so sad
and I'm still hurting

Gave up on a lover
can't figure out friends
It's life on life's terms
a means to an end

—Jeff West

17

Deepening Your Awareness

CONSCIOUSLY living your life is *your birth-right*. Yet the long-term effects of substance use will cloud your experience in a haze of confusion, illusion, self-doubt, self-hate, self-sabotage, distrust in your ability to heal, and a determination to escape from your life situation. *Sustaining your recovery* is about deepening your awareness that *all of your life experiences are benefiting you*.

Here are the main points explored in this chapter. I encourage you to entertain these concepts from the perspective of *'What if it is true?'* Check ☑ those that are most significant for your recovery or that you have questions or concerns about.

☐ Utilizing all of your senses, including your intuition, facilitates awareness.

☐ Developing your awareness facilitates your transformation.

☐ Greater awareness will help you maximize your experiences.

☐ Increasing your awareness cultivates greater understanding.

☐ There is no limit to how much you can develop your awareness.

☐ Your awareness is your ability to focus your attention and tune into what is happening.

☐ Your awareness has a direct impact on illuminating and changing your reality.

☐ Coupling your intention with your attention deepens your awareness.

☐ Mindfulness practices (breathing, acceptance, non-judgment, opening your heart, non-attachment, presence) cultivate your awareness.

☐ Your awareness is the ongoing practice of becoming more conscious.

☐ You can develop your awareness with practice.

☐ Your awareness assists you to derive benefits from all of the insights, gifts, and lessons that are offered.

WE can see the Divine
in each speck of dust,
but that doesn't stop us
from wiping it away
with a wet sponge.
The Divine doesn't disappear;
it's transformed
into the clean surface.

—Paulo Coelho

YOUR awareness is a quality of your natural *state of being* as distinguished from your *doing*. Your awareness is the result of *being present in your life*. It is your tuning into the 'here-and-now' of what is *actually* happening. You experience awareness on a continuum. Indeed, many factors, including your

* energy level
* ability to focus
* receptivity
* anxiety
* worrying
* insecurity
* perceptions
* conditioning

contribute to *increasing* or *decreasing* your awareness from moment to moment.

Your awareness allows you to stay grounded by assisting your human self to

* identify your *responsibilities*
* make well-informed *choices* and decisions
* follow your *intuition*
* keep in the forefront the needs of *both* your soul and your human self.

Focusing Your Intentions

Your intentions direct your awareness. You will want to develop the habit of being present to your intentions in all of your interactions, including your intentions for yourself. *Clarity on your intentions* allows you to co-create what you desire to manifest. To focus your intentions, ask yourself the following questions and check ☑ those you answer 'Yes':

☐ Do I want to *enjoy* the company of others?

☐ Do I want to be *a unifying force?*

☐ Do I want to be my own *best friend* and ally?

☐ Do I want to *face* my fears?

☐ Do I want to be *empowered?*

☐ Do I want to derive *the greatest benefit* from my experiences?

☐ Do I want to access and meet *both* my human needs *and* my soul needs?

☐ Do I want to *experience* enjoyment, happiness, balance, passion, vitality, fun, play, meaning, purpose, serenity, connection, and fulfillment?

Your intentions will focus your mind in a particular way. You can then determine whether these are beneficial or harmful. *The more you focus on some aspect of your reality, the more aware you become.*

Reality is defined as what is taking place in the framework of your mental processing, emotions, body sensations, intuition, and experiences.

Your degree of awareness has a direct impact on your ability to change your reality. When you find yourself judging someone and become aware of it, resolve instead to be *a unifying presence*. When you open your heart, the energy exchange will become qualitatively different.

Coupling your intention with your attention deepens your awareness. There you discover the insights, gifts, and lessons within your experiences. Integrating these will allow you to modify your ways of thinking, which will then change your external reality.

If you choose awareness as a guiding practice, *your life will take on a deeper sense of meaning and purpose.* Increasing your awareness gives you access to 'the bigger picture' as well as to your life calling.

Consciously Living Your Life

You are *intended* to have *conscious living experiences*. You can become increasingly aware of being conscious in all your experiences.

If your mind is saying that being present is too much work, the truth is that *it requires even more time, energy, and work* when you are not present in your life. Why? Because the less present you are, the more you are *missing out* on what is actually happening in the moment.

Check ☑ the benefits of *becoming more present* that you would like to experience:

☐ having *more time* to linger in the enjoyable moments

☐ identifying and *integrating* all the insights, gifts, and lessons you are offered

☐ being *empowered* in all your relationships

☐ making conscious and well-informed *choices and decisions*

☐ keeping your head and *energy field* clear

☐ identifying and meeting both *your human and soul needs* more effectively

☐ being *nourished* energetically

☐ experiencing more *wisdom, enjoyment, vitality, pleasure, courage, hope, connection,* and *satisfaction*.

Your ability to be present will not be perfect, but you can *improve with practice*.

Everything you do is of significance, which is why you want to *stay fully present* in your life. Developing your awareness is the lifelong practice of becoming increasingly more present. Greater awareness, both internally and externally, will help you connect the dots in whatever you do. Being aware will shine a light on how you are *co-creating your reality* every day.

You develop your awareness by *staying present in your experiencing and utilizing your five senses* (sight, hearing, touch, smell, and taste) *as well as your intuition* (your sixth or 'soul' sense). The more you become aware, the more you will see, feel, hear, taste, and intuit. If any of your senses becomes impaired, the other ones will compensate by becoming more proficient at what they do.

The practice of awareness is about *'being with'* and *'tuning into'* your experiences. Being aware helps you experience all aspects of your reality more fully. Increasing your awareness will deepen your understanding of how you want to live your life as well as your willingness to take responsibility for everything that happens to you.

Developing Your Mindfulness Skills

Along with your physical senses, the so-called *mindfulness practices* are some of the most effective ways to develop awareness. Utilizing these skills will facilitate your becoming more present in general as well as more aware of what you are actually experiencing. Here's what to do:

❖ *stay present* in the 'here-and-now'

❖ stay in tune with your *breath*

❖ *accept* what is happening (this does not mean you have to like it)

❖ try your best to be *nonjudgmental*

❖ remain *open-hearted*

❖ remain *open-minded*

❖ let go of any *attachment* to outcomes.

You are training your ***mind*** to become aware, not your soul. These mindfulness practices have been proven to produce positive results.

❖ ***Developing presence*** trains your mind to slow down and fosters merging your human self with your soul.

❖ ***Breathing*** brings oxygen to your physical body, focuses your mind, and fosters relaxation.

❖ ***Accepting*** assists your mind to stay present with what is happening rather than trying to resist it, helps you own all aspects of your reality, and allows others to have theirs.

❖ ***Being nonjudgmental*** prevents your human self from relating to others from a one-up or one-down position, and also helps you accept your imperfections and derive greater benefit from your experiences.

❖ ***Maintaining an open heart*** nurtures your human self, increases your self-esteem, and raises your energy level.

❖ ***Having an open mind*** keeps your mental defenses from getting in the way and allows your intellect to be receptive to and gain access to insights, gifts, and lessons being offered in your experiences.

❖ ***Being unattached*** assists your mind to embrace change, deepens your understanding of life cycles, and helps you remain grounded.

Deepening Your Awareness

It is *your birthright* to live your life consciously. Your awareness will increase exponentially as your intellect becomes more aligned with your soul. *It is your mind that has to yield to and merge with your soul, not the other way around.* You can develop your awareness to become more conscious in your daily experiences.

The more conscious you become, the greater *access* you will have to all the insights, gifts, and lessons that are always being offered. They are intended to assist you to *deepen* your understanding of everything that is happening in your life. This will require staying *grounded* by taking full responsibility for your life.

Living up to your full potential is about accomplishing *your soul mission* or calling in life. If part of your soul mission is to be a mother or father, the importance of this role will be illuminated in light of how it is benefiting you. As you move forward you can rest assured that more will always be revealed.

Deepening your awareness will facilitate accessing *your truth* and illuminate the answers to your questions.

The voice of your conscience is your soul's knowing. Have you ever wondered about the *conflicts* in your mind? They may be the result of your mind bumping up against the *limitations* of your conditioning or going against the *prompting* of your best interests. Developing self-awareness is the key to resolving these conflicts and accessing your soul's wisdom.

Awareness and Your Direct Experience

Although intellectual understanding is important and necessary, *your direct experience makes an indelible impression on your mind* and allows your human self to merge with your soul. Your experiences and insights inform your knowing, and your knowing cannot be denied.

Having an experience and *being aware* of having that experience are not the same: the former is often limited to going through the motions, while the latter means *tuning into* the details of the 'here-and-now.'

Your awareness will assist you to derive the most *benefit* from your experiences by helping you identify what is being offered.

Changing Your Conditioning

Awareness is a means of *deepening* your experiences of reality. The more fully you experience what is occurring internally as well as externally, the greater your understanding.

With practice you can develop your awareness to laser beam-like precision. Your awareness informs your perceptions, which in turn directly influence your conditioning: the beliefs and thought patterns with which your mind identifies.

The rightful position of your human self is to be *the agent* of your soul. Living in Alignment is about *reprogramming your mind to listen to your soul* and follow its directives. Your human self is intended to serve as the *vehicle* or hands and feet of your soul. This partnership cannot be forced; instead it must be developed.

You have been taught to rely on your intellect to direct your life. When you depend primarily on logical, linear, and rational ways of thinking, *becoming internally resourced is not easy*. The more cerebral you become (keeping your mind in the driver's seat), the more difficult it will be to experience Living in Alignment with your soul.

Reprogramming your mind to be in service of your soul may be *threatening* to your ego. It is the part of your mind that thinks it is a separate entity that has to *maintain control* of your human self.

Soul realization is the acknowledgment that at your core you are a unique aspect of Source energy, and that you are both separate and one at the same time.

It is important to *normalize* any resistance your mind may have about becoming internally resourced.

Living in Alignment is a *state of being* and something you *experience*, whereas intellectualizing is a step removed from your experience.

Choosing Not to Become Aware

One of the reasons you may choose **not** to develop your awareness is that when you experience anything less than being nurtured, your human self instinctively gets **triggered** and goes into **survival mode**. You may erect mental and emotional barriers involving anger, denial, and avoidance or use other coping strategies to deal with perceived threats to your wellbeing. As a result you may live in **fight-or-flight mode** or **dissociate** from stressful experiences.

If you are not very present in such circumstances, and thus less aware of the details of your experiences, you will **miss out on a lot of what is being offered**.

All of your experiences have the **inherent potential** of benefiting you. This includes not only those that are enjoyable, but also those you experience as **traumatic**. You may **close down** when you get triggered. This is an inadequate coping strategy to prevent further assault. When this happens, your brain goes into a startled or *'freeze'* response that keeps you functioning in the sympathetic fight-or-flight mode, and you become **stuck in your 'story'** (the drama you are experiencing).

If, however, you embrace the idea that **all of your experiences are benefiting you**, while you also work on

❖ establishing and maintaining healthy **boundaries**

❖ **allowing** others to have their realities

❖ identifying and getting *your human and soul needs* met

❖ living in *moderation* (creating balance and harmony in your life)

❖ developing *self-esteem*

❖ learning to be more *assertive*

you will be better prepared to deal effectively with whatever happens in your life.

Identifying and working through your unresolved *trauma-related issues* will reduce your *triggering episodes* and help you be less *defensive*. The more internally resourced you become, the *safer* being in the world will feel to your human self.

Developing your awareness is more difficult if you have not learned a *process* for becoming more aware. It requires having a *skill base* that you can develop. As you become aware of the benefits of living consciously, you will become more inspired and motivated to develop your awareness skills. Becoming more aware *facilitates your self-empowerment.*

Finally, you may have avoided becoming more aware because you did not want to take *full responsibility* for your life. By remaining stuck in *'victim mode'* you may be receiving a lot of *secondary gains*. Or the primary support people in your life may be enabling or *colluding* with you (often unknowingly) to stay stuck.

As a result, you become *less and less empowered* when you avoid taking responsibility for your life. The good news is that *in moments of insight* your human self can *decide* to take responsibility for your life. You can then access your soul's *guidance* on how to reclaim your life and your power.

Practicing Your Awareness

Becoming aware will increase with practice. Disciplining your mind to focus is an integral part of this ongoing process. You develop this capacity by *focusing on the task at hand.* It doesn't matter what the task is. Assign all tasks equal importance and approach them with thoughtfulness and attention.

Your mind will tend to wander here, there, and everywhere. This is to be expected until your mind develops the capacity to direct your attention. *Normalizing the wanderings of your mind* will foster an acceptance of what is. Avoid judging, blaming, shaming, or getting mad at yourself for this behavior.

Instead, use the fact that your mind is wandering as a cue to come back and *focus* on the task. With practice you will become better at focusing. Becoming aware requires focusing on the *'here-and-now,'* on the *'what-and-how'* of your experiencing. It is your task to keep your mind on track and avoid distractions.

Awareness Facilitates Your Transformation

If you're walking around with *blinders* on or just *going through the motions* of your life, you will miss out on a lot of things.

Awareness is a skill that can be developed and a practice intended to *illuminate* your life. Instead of denying, compartmentalizing, dissociating, avoiding, ignoring, minimizing, or completely rejecting aspects of yourself and your reality, you can develop awareness skills that will help you become more accepting of what is *really* happening in your life.

Learning to *linger in these moments* is very important, for in so doing you gain the ability to *identify, receive,* and *integrate* what is being offered to you. The more you become aware, the more conscious you are of the *choices* and *opportunities* that are always before you. With increased awareness you will come to know the *benefits* of Living in Alignment in the context of your daily life. Likewise, with greater awareness you will also have a better sense of when you're *off track* and 'get it' sooner rather than later.

Awareness is *a crucial aspect of your transformational process*. When your awareness is coupled with your intention to experience greater union with yourself and all life forms, *your journey of awakening accelerates*.

All of your experiences and life circumstances have the *inherent potential* of benefiting you, but unless you *tune into* the specifics of what is happening in your life, you will not gain any insights. Tuning in requires that you be present, and presence requires awareness.

Here's how your awareness directly impacts co-creating your reality and facilitates transformation. As you tune into the

1. *concept* that every experience is benefiting you, coupled with the

2. *intention* to open your mind to the specifics of how this is so, along with your

3. *presence* and

4. *focus* (tuning into what is), you gain

5. *access* to the insights, gifts, and lessons being offered. Your task is to

6. *integrate* them into your life. Doing so

7. *deepens* your understanding, which

8. *transforms* some aspect of your life, which in turn

9. *increases* your awareness even more.

> YOU will know the truth,
> and the truth will make you free.
> —John 8:32

Being Externally Resourced vs. Being Aware

When you are primarily *externally resourced* you miss out on so much that is happening in your life. You are ruled by outside influences, living in fear-based reality, and stuck in survival mode. Check ☑ the facts of your life experience:

☐ Your awareness is focused on taking care of your *basic needs* (food, clothing, shelter, financial stability, medical care, sexual pleasure).

☐ You are preoccupied with *a lack of resources*, thinking that you cannot trust people, that you have to keep your defenses up, that life is a struggle and then you die, that you are defective, that your life is about repenting for your sins, and that Source energy is a judging, menacing, punishing force.

☐ You become *obsessed* with experiencing your life from a *dualistic* perspective: good/bad, right/wrong, positive/negative, winner/loser.

Attending to your survival needs is absolutely necessary. But is just surviving enough? You may realize that living in a *fear-based* reality is no longer an option. You want to *thrive* instead of just surviving.

You have Choices about How to Live

The good news is that *you can choose how you want to live your life.* The old model of deepening in relationship was about *self-sacrifice* to the point of neglecting your human needs, living in deprivation or poverty mode, associating hardship and suffering with virtue, and staying in adversarial, unsupportive, or otherwise non-nurturing conditions and/or relationships.

You can take responsibility to claim your life and can choose how you want to evolve. Our new understanding is that we evolve through enjoyment, awareness, pleasure, passion, satisfaction, love, connection, and fulfillment. And because these are states of being that *increase* your energy level, you will also develop your *capacity* to live in these states.

You will learn to discern which ways of thinking and behaviors are *sabotaging* you or preventing you from experiencing these energy states. To attract them, keep your intention focused on the *opportunities* being offered within your experiences.

THE Hasidic sage Rabbi Susya
once said to a companion,
"When I reach the next world,
God will not ask me,
'Why were you not Moses?'
God will ask me,
'Why were you not Rabbi Susya?
Why were you not the person
I created you to be?'"

—Martin Buber

18

The Living in Alignment Model

THE Living in Alignment Model has one primary purpose: to assist you to *discover and experience* Source energy within yourself and in your life. In so doing you will find the direct link to realizing your true desires and creating a life that is filled with possibilities that are truly awesome, attainable, gratifying, and transformative!

The Living in Alignment approach is intended to

- ❖ *bridge* the gap between science and spirituality
- ❖ foster your *integrity*
- ❖ facilitate your personal *transformation*
- ❖ offer concepts that *expand* your awareness
- ❖ assist you to *live* authentically
- ❖ facilitate your living up to your greatest *potential*
- ❖ illuminate the *significance* of your life
- ❖ *deepen* your connection with Source energy
- ❖ discover and *actualize* your soul mission
- ❖ access Source energy *directly*
- ❖ *illuminate* how you are co-creating your life with Source energy
- ❖ keep your *egoic* mind from getting in your way

❖ assist you to move out of fear- and ***shame***-based realities

❖ foster ***unity*** consciousness

❖ facilitate your ***grounding*** in the physical world

❖ assist you to appreciate and ***embrace*** your humanity

❖ assist you to reclaim your ***power*** from people, behaviors, conditions, and events etc.

Living in Alignment is intended as a ***comprehensive*** approach, either to augment and complement your existing resources or to help you design your own individualized spiritual practice.

The aim and distinguishing feature of the Living in Alignment Model is to foster a ***partnership*** between your human self and your soul (or Source energy within).

The methods utilized in the Living in Alignment process are derived from the author's personal experiences, many spiritual traditions, and various therapeutic modalities (such as Cognitive Behavioral, Solution-focused, Psychodynamic, Psycho-spiritual, Transpersonal, Humanistic, Gestalt) that have been ***integrated*** in working with the recovery community in residential and outpatient settings.

The Living in Alignment approach will assist you to become more ***aware*** of the workings of Source energy in your life and to ***awaken*** you to the wonders of living in your human form.

The Living in Alignment perspective affirms that you are intended to *be your own expert* when it comes to *knowing* what your deepest needs, wants, and desires are and what will offer you meaning and purpose in your life.

Living in Alignment is a *lifelong practice* of becoming increasingly more present and aware of the experiences you are having, the significance of your life, and the roles you take on.

Living in Alignment is *a state of being* and living in the world that is *in harmony* with universal energy principles.

Living in Alignment will increase your energy level. It will have a *synergistic effect* on your optimal functioning, yielding an overall sense of well-being and the most favorable results.

The information and skill base presented in the Living in Alignment Model is designed to assist your human self in *getting out of your way*. In developing a partnership with your soul, your mind is listening to and following your soul's guidance and prompting. When this occurs, Living in Alignment becomes a reality, along with the experience of discovering *'freedom to be'* all of who you are.

Living in Alignment moves you out of a *'me'* mentality to an *'us'* framework/perspective, illuminating the reality that everyone is *interconnected* and *interdependent*, and that your presence is intended to *make a difference* in people's lives — to truly benefit others and vice versa.

Living in Alignment is an *alternative way of being* and living your life that offers both short- and long-term benefits. These benefits are experienced whenever you listen to and follow the guidance/prompting from your soul.

Living in Alignment is a *practical, effective,* and *trustworthy* approach to *sustaining* your recovery:

❖ *practical:* Living in Alignment is user-friendly, attainable, and realistic.

❖ *effective:* Living in Alignment is well-founded, useful, powerful, sound, beneficial, and valuable.

❖ *trustworthy:* Living in Alignment is reliable, dependable, can be subjectively validated, and will stand the test of time.

Are you ready to consider Living in Alignment? Check ☑ if your answer to these questions is *'Yes!'*

☐ Are you committed to staying *clean and sober?*

☐ Do you desire to get *unstuck* and *thrive* in your recovery?

☐ Do you want to experience *authentic living?*

☐ Do you seek to become *self-empowered?*

☐ Is your goal to live up to your *full potential?*

☐ Are you interested in dealing with your *guilt, shame,* and *fear?*

☐ Are you ready for *personal transformation?*

☐ Are you longing to experience *self-acceptance* and heal from past and current *wounding?*

☐ Do you want to deepen your *relationship* with Source energy (or a Power greater than your mind)?

☐ Are you ready to *discover* your soul connection?

Resources for Living in Alignment

Living in Alignment is a comprehensive approach to *sustainable recovery* that you can incorporate into your plan to stay clean and sober and design your personal spiritual practice.

Living in Alignment was developed through the author's professional work on staff of The Meadows of Wickenburg, AZ, the Life Healing Center of Santa Fe, NM, Focus Treatment Center and Valley Recovery Center of Sacramento, CA, as well as in his private practice with clients in recovery.

The Living in Alignment approach is designed to be integrated into holistic treatment plans developed by residential treatment centers and intensive outpatient programs, and is also offered by licensed and certified practitioners in private practice.

For more information on the Living in Alignment program, resources, events, and practitioners, or to join the Living in Alignment Community on line, visit:

www.LivingInAlignment.ca

THE JOURNEY

One day you finally knew
What you had to do, and began,
Though the voices around you
Kept shouting
Their bad advice —
> Though the whole house began to tremble
> And you felt the old tug
> At your ankles.
> 'Mend my life!'
> Each voice cried.
> But you didn't stop.
You knew what you had to do,
Though the wind pried
With its stiff fingers
At the very foundations,
Though their melancholy
Was terrible.
> It was already late
> Enough, and a wild night,
> And the road full of fallen
> Branches and stones.
But little by little,
As you left their voices behind,
The stars began to burn
Through the sheets of clouds,
> And there was a new voice
> Which you slowly
> Recognized as your own,
> That kept you company
> As you strode deeper and deeper
> Into the world,
Determined to do
The only thing you could do —
Determined to save
The only life you could save.
>   —Mary Oliver

A

Relationship Issues and Dependence

RESEARCH studies have confirmed that receiving *consistent emotional nurturance* is an *absolute requirement* for healthy neurobiological brain development and maintenance. This is especially true during your early or formative years in order for your human self to become emotionally present/available with yourself and with others throughout your lifespan. *The lack of emotional attunement and consistently available parenting figures* is a major source of stress for children.

You may have developed *attachment issues* as a child if the nurturing from your major caregivers was *inadequate*. This includes *insufficient* nurturing around your inherent worth; protecting yourself; accepting your human reality; your needs/wants; and regulating your energy. When this occurs, your drive *to pursue and preserve intimacy* with yourself, with others, and with Source energy is challenged.

Unfavorable/harmful *peer influence* during your vulnerable teen years (or in any other stage of your life) can also have an adverse impact on your overall health and wellbeing.

Other studies have found that *favorable/nurturing experiences* lead to healthy brain development while the *absence* of these experiences or the presence of harmful/unhealthy ones distorts development in essential brain structures.

For example, *poorly attuned childhood relationships* (in which you don't feel seen, understood, accepted, empathized with, 'gotten' on the emotional level, and loved as an individual) provide *an inadequate template* for the development of neurological and psychological self-regulation systems. This can lead to mood, anxiety, and other mental disorders, various immune disorders, and becomes *the biological basis for chemical imbalances* in your brain that can predispose you to becoming dependent upon mood-altering substances or behaviors.

Inadequate nurturing around your *inherent worth* can lead to poor self-regulation and an inability to self-soothe. When this occurs, you will tend to *look outside yourself for emotional soothing.* This can translate to becoming susceptible to *the lure of instant gratification* that psychotropic substances or behavioral addictions offer. When you achieve *healthy self-regulation*, you will not experience rapidly shifting extremes of emotional highs and lows in the face of life's challenges, difficulties, disappointments, and dissatisfactions.

Although it is important to keep in the forefront that *loving parents are doing the best they can with what they know*, it is also true that their best parenting skills can be *inadequate*. In addition, parents will pass on to their children whatever they don't deal with in their own lives.

I call your attention to the correlation between inadequate nurturing, attachment issues, and substance-related disorders because of its relevance to your recovery process. *Your healing process is about transforming the circumstances of your past and current life.* This involves identifying what you need to heal and learning to *give yourself the nurturance* that was (or still is) lacking.

The Living in Alignment approach will *assist you to develop a loving/nurturing relationship with your human self and embrace your humanity*. Learning to open your heart to yourself and become your own best friend and ally has a *direct impact* on balancing your brain chemistry, forming healthy and satisfying relationships with yourself and others, living up to your full potential, and thriving in your recovery.

T HOSE whom we call addicts
are simply intense seekers of bliss
who have gotten stuck in repetition,
looking for the right thing in the wrong place.
When we let go of the self-image
we used to identify with, we find behind it
the experience of unity we've been seeking.

—Amrit Desai

187

TRANSFORMATION
It will not always feel good,
This growing.
This stretching beyond the boundaries of the known,
The comfortable.

It will not always feel safe,
This learning and relearning of your own abilities
This reexamining of beliefs
This pushing of envelopes
This breaking through enclosing walls.

You will shiver.
You will doubt.
You will want to run home.
Back behind walls of safety.

This walk to the edge will not
Feel good, safe, or comfortable,
But there is no faster way to learn.
There is no other way to grow.

So step out.
Leave your home base
Your comfort zone
Your cocoon
Acknowledge the fear and discomfort
But step out all the same.

With each step you take,
Your world expands
Your caterpillar mind will
Strain to comprehend the unbounded vastness of the sky.

Step out.
Step…step…step.
Unfurl your wings.
Fly.

—Meg Goodmanson

B

Are You Living in Alignment or Just Surviving?

FROM the perspective of Living in Alignment, your ego represents that aspect of your mind that thinks your experience of *being a separate self* is all there is. Your ego is also viewed as the *instinctual aspect* of the human organism that is programmed to satisfy your survival needs and maintain stability. The more you are externally re-sourced, the more you think and live as though your human self is *entirely separate* and view the three-dimensional world before your eyes as *all there is* to life.

A key insight in the Living in Alignment Model is that *we are both human and spiritual beings*, not one or the other. Living in Alignment views your human self as being both separate and at the same time one with Source energy.

Your Experience of Being Primarily Externally Resourced

When you identify with the perception that your human self is *a separate entity*, your *intellect* will tend to become your point of reference. From the perspective of Living in Alignment, your intellect is simply *the sum total of your conditioning* (familial, religious, educational, and political). When your intellect becomes your main point of reference, your human self is inclined to allow societal conditioning to take precedence and govern your life. ***When your self-understanding is defined by your intellect you become primarily externally resourced.***

Disconnecting from Your Soul

The more you become externally resourced, the less you are **connected to your soul and to the world of Mystery**. The more you are externally resourced, the more difficulty you will likely have in opening to the concept that **you have a soul**, let alone in being receptive to becoming internally resourced (deferring to your soul for guidance).

The less you are connected to your soul, the more **insecure** your human self feels with itself, with others, with being on Planet Earth, and in living your life. Consequently, the less you are connected with your soul, the more your human self will live in a **fear-** or **shame**-based reality. Until your human self becomes internally resourced, you will have **limited access** to universal wisdom and 'the bigger picture' of your life: that all your experiences benefit you.

Societal Conditioning and Shame-based Reality

When you are primarily externally resourced, your reference point for viewing and experiencing your life is restricted by your **societal conditioning**. Because the **socialization process** uses shaming as a way to control and manipulate people to conform to conventional standards, the more externally re-sourced you become, the more likely it is that you will live in a *shame-based reality*.

Until the direct and indirect shaming messages you receive from your social interactions are questioned, challenged, and discarded as needed, they invariably become *internalized*. As a result, you may find yourself habitually shaming yourself (including put-downs, ridiculing, judging, fault-finding, blaming, etc.).

The Dominance of Your Intellect

When your human self is primarily externally resourced, *your intellect becomes the manager of your personality*. (In this context 'personality' refers to all the components of your human self: your physical body, your behaviors, your emotions, your beliefs and ways of thinking.) Your intellect is primarily (if not solely) concerned with and focused on your human needs and wants—without recognizing that your soul has needs as well.

Furthermore, your human self becomes *ego centered* when you think that you are neither interconnected with nor interdependent with other people and life forms. When you look around, you can see this being played out by many people who are *self-centered, self-seeking, conceited* and the like.

From the perspective of Living in Alignment, *your intellect is like a computer, and your beliefs and thinking patterns are the software*. Thus you are free to modify, change, or replace your conditioning. This process is referred to as ***deprogramming*** and ***reprogramming***.

Deferring to Your Soul

From the perspective of Living in Alignment, your human self, including your intellect, is ***intended to function as the agent of your soul***. This translates to your human self ***deferring*** to your soul for directives and ***working in unison*** with your soul to accomplish your calling in life in any particular lifetime.

Once your human self ***recognizes*** that your soul is more capable of being at the helm, so to speak, and ***experiences the benefits*** of listening to and following its prompting (a deep sense of mental relief and ease; greater success, meaning, and purpose; balance, vitality, and courage; increased awareness; sustainable happiness and contentment; placing your human needs and your best interests in the forefront; continuously offering guidance and providing opportunities; absence of fear; increased self esteem; accessing your calling in life), you will both ***yearn*** and ***endeavor*** to become internally resourced and to be Living in Alignment.

A Shift in Orientation

What if your life is intended to be ***a transformative adventure?*** From the perspective of Living in Alignment, not only is this concept believable, it is also a viable way to live your life, and better still is both reliable and testable. Becoming internally re-sourced is literally *a change in your life's orientation*, as you learn to defer to your soul for guidance rather than allowing the conditioning of your human self or societal dictates to be the overriding factor.

Synchronicity, Providence, and Destiny

The more you become internally resourced and are Living in Alignment, the more *you actually experience the workings of your soul in your daily life*. As you develop your awareness, you become increasingly conscious of your soul's activity.

Your soul is *ingenious* and *highly creative* in the countless ways it works with your human self. Your human self will be *absolutely amazed* at some of the workings of your soul within your life and the lives of others.

As you become more internally resourced and begin Living in Alignment, you become more aware of *how you participate in the co-creation of your life,* where synchronicity, providence, and destiny play out in astonishing ways.

Becoming internally resourced is a shift in your awareness from a dominant ego to soul realization. As you develop your intuitive sense, you will con-sciously participate in the *evolutionary transition* from being a five-sensory being to becoming a six-sensory (intuitive) being.

An integral aspect of the Living in Alignment

process is examining all of your beliefs, in that your beliefs and thinking patterns are viewed as a *lens* through which you see and *filter* out information that becomes the basis for co-creating your reality.

Transforming Black-and-White Thinking

It is also apparent that the more externally re-sourced you become, the more you live your life in dualism. In other words, you see and experience life through a black-and-white lens or *limiting view of reality* that categorizes everything as good or bad, right or wrong, positive or negative.

As you become more internally resourced, you will experience *less dualism* and realize how all life circumstances are benefiting you. Instead of catas-trophizing, judging, or jumping to conclusions, you will develop an open mind, accept what is happen-ing, and trust that more shall be revealed on an as-needed basis.

In addition, what at first appeared as *paradoxical* (such as the truth that we are both separate and one at the same time) becomes increasingly clear and makes more sense.

The Living in Alignment approach offers con-cepts intended to open your mind and expand your individual consciousness to access universal wis-dom. These are offered from a *'What if it is true?'* perspective.

This is a deliberate means to assist your mind to avoid becoming *defensive* and automatically *reject-*

ing other information that challenges your conditioning. From a 'What if it is true?' perspective, the concepts presented in the Living in Alignment Model are understood as *working hypotheses*, intended to be tested in your life experience.

Having direct or subjective experiences of these concepts allows you to move from a place of disbelief, or believing (or wanting to believe) something is so, to a place of *knowing intuitively that it is so*.

L IFE is an opportunity: benefit from it.
Life is beauty: admire it.
Life is a dream: realize it.

Life is a challenge: meet it.
Life is a duty: complete it.
Life is a game: play it.

Life is a promise: fulfill it.
Life is sorrow: overcome it.
Life is a song: sing it.

Life is a struggle: accept it.
Life is a tragedy: confront it.
Life is an adventure: dare it.

Life is luck: make it.
Life is too precious: do not destroy it.
Life is life: fight for it.

—Mother Teresa

TO be considered heaven
or to be considered hell,
I have lived it.
Was it a journey
or was it a trap?

> The question stays unanswered but
> the answer ultimately relies
> on the way I view it.

While in the middle of the chaos
I thought I was suffering
but when I am able to look at my life now,
I was called.

> Everyone's destination has a purpose,
> has a spirit that needs to be lifted.

When I saw you I knew why I was here every time.
I thought I was losing my mind,
but I was experiencing a life of creation
I had no idea existed.

> The stories, the people, the scenery
> was the way I learned to live.

And when it was completed
and a heart was healed,
I was on to the next.

> The life seems crazy and
> to me I was ashamed.

But today to know there was a reason
to all the madness, to help a soul
shows me the true reason I am on this earth.

> I am here for you,
> the time has come,
> was it heaven
> or was it hell?

—Brianna Pfiester

C

How to Stay Present

FROM the perspective of Living in Alignment, your human self is intended to be a *clear channel* for your soul as well as to serve as its hands and feet. Your task is thus to 'stay present' to your experience in the moment. The more present you are, the more conscious you become.

Your interactions with your human self, with other people, and with all life forms offer *insights, gifts, and lessons* for living your life. Bringing increased awareness to your experiences requires focusing your attention and intention on *staying present*. The practice of staying present facilitates becoming internally resourced and Living in Alignment.

The following suggestions can help you *stay present*. Keep in mind that the objective is *not* to do it perfectly, but to do the best you can to be present with yourself, with others, and with your experiences. Remember that practice makes better.

1. *Breathe consciously* ~ to clear your mind and direct your attention to being in your body.

2. *Identify how you tend to 'numb out'* ~ to help your human self own *all* aspects of your reality (mental emotional, physical, spiritual, and be-

haviors). These include substance and process addictions; walls of words, silence, anger, fear; selective hearing and seeing; denial; overdoing/ staying busy; isolation; being emotionally absent; and mental defenses.

3. *Accept what is happening* ~ to focus your mind on the 'here-and-now'.

4. Embrace the concept that *'all circumstances have the inherent potential of benefiting you'* ~ to be receptive to your experience.

5. Keep in the forefront that *'your presence and your life are of significance'* ~ to reassure your human self and keep your mind from 'spacing out'.

6. Allow your *resistance* to be your cue ~ *to accept what is* and remind your human self that you are not being present to what is happening.

7. *Avoid taking on other people's realities* ~ to prevent yourself from being overwhelmed and assuming the responsibilities of others.

8. Be careful *not to get caught up in the story* (yours or others') ~ to help your human self maintain balance and regulate your energy.

9. Tune into how *others are being catalysts for you* ~ to focus your mind on how this is so, and thus keep your attention on your experience.

10. Pay attention to how *you are a catalyst for others* ~ to help yourself focus your attention on

specific tasks.

11. Establish and maintain *healthy external boundaries* ~ to protect yourself from others who may not be Living in Alignment and give yourself more confidence and a feeling of ease when interacting with others.

12. Establish and maintain *healthy internal boundaries* ~ to help ensure that your human self/intellect does not sabotage your best interests or those of others.

13. Utilize your *assertiveness skills* ~ to keep yourself empowered.

14. *Move from a literal interpretation* of your experience *to the symbolic* ~ to help your human self gain insights, gifts, and lessons.

15. *Avoid comparing your journey with others* (as better-than or less-than) ~ to focus your attention on being present with all the transitions occurring in your life.

16. Focus on *what you want to manifest* (vs. emphasizing what you don't want) ~ to develop the skill of combining your intention with attention to your experience.

17. Listen to *hear what people are saying* (including reading between the lines) ~ to tune into being present with others and what is happening in their realities.

18. Ask for *clarification* when needed ~ to stay pre-

sent and avoid misunderstandings in your interactions with others.

19. Always ***put your best foot forward*** in whatever you do ~ to focus on the task at hand.

20. ***Be present*** to your experience of the *'here-and-now'* ~ to help your human self tune into the insights, gifts, and lessons being offered in your reality.

21. ***Learn from making 'mistakes'*** ~ to focus your attention on expanding your awareness.

22. ***Own all aspects of your reality*** (what you are experiencing, thinking, feeling, and intuiting) ~ to be fully present to what is happening.

23. Tune into your experiences ~ to ***recognize insights, gifts, and lessons*** and focus on expanding your awareness.

24. Tune into your experiences ~ to ***discern opportunities*** to be open to ***all*** the experiences you are intended to have.

25. ***Keep your energy field clear*** ~ to stay present and focused.

26. ***Say what you mean and mean what you say*** ~ to stay empowered in your relationships with others.

27. Identify and ***take care of your human and soul needs*** ~ to grasp that all the experiences you are having are intended to illuminate and meet ***all*** your needs.

28. *Be solution-focused* ~ to reprogram your human self and deepen your capacity to direct your attention and join it with your intention.

29. *'Let go and let God'* ~ to release your grip on needing to know *why* things happen the way they do and to *trust* that more shall always be revealed on an as-needed basis. This practice helps train your human self to *feel into your life* (versus trying to figure it out). In so doing you become more relaxed and open to your experiences.

30. *Try not to take what is happening personally* ~ to train yourself not to take on or blame yourself for other peoples' realities.

31. *Lighten up* ~ to help your human self enjoy your experiences.

32. *Offer yourself tender loving care* ~ to comfort your human self and be more at ease with yourself and your life.

33. *Keep your heart and mind open* to yourself and others ~ to increase your energy level.

34. *Break down tasks* into manageable/enjoyable steps ~ to avoid becoming overwhelmed with your earthly responsibilities, and thus become more present in everything you do.

35. *Be careful not to become overwhelmed* ~ to regulate your energy in your daily experience.

36. *Find the 'right' balance* in your life ~ to gain

the most benefit from your experiences.

37. ***Don't abandon your human self*** or your journey ~ to allow your mind to grasp the significance of your experiences.

38. Make a commitment to be ***part of the solution*** (vs. part of the problem) ~ to help your mind focus your energy.

39. Be proactive about ***doing what needs to get done*** ~ to focus your mind on completing specific tasks.

40. Give your human self ***reassuring talks*** ~ to offer support/encouragement and prevent your mind from getting stuck, 'spacing out', or going into despair.

41. ***Become your own best friend and ally*** ~ to help your human self do the right thing.

42. ***Normalize what is happening*** in the interplay of your human self and Source energy ~ to remind yourself of 'the bigger picture' of your life.

43. ***Be authentic*** in your interactions ~ to keep yourself empowered.

44. Monitor ***your energy expenditure*** (including your activities, foods you eat, people you associate with, organizations you are affiliated with) ~ to help your human self stay in balance.

45. ***Enjoy yourself*** and your life ~ to receive the benefit of what is being offered.

46. ***Hold yourself accountable*** ~ to remind yourself

that you are interconnected with and interdependent with other people and all life forms and that your presence has an impact.

47. *Stay calm* ~ to assist yourself to be more present in your experiences.

48. Develop *a sense of humor* ~ to help yourself enjoy your daily life.

49. Receive *the love being offered* ~ to increase your energy level and make your life more enjoyable and rewarding.

50. Avoid *judging* yourself or others ~ to accept what is happening in the moment and promote your 'freedom to be'.

51. Be careful *not to jump to conclusions* ~ to stay present with what is happening and allow the process to unfold.

MY Sweet Necessity
Nothing so cherished
It has become me
Passing my lips
A kind of necessity
It guides my thoughts
Stays in my dreams
It's there for me
It's necessary
A pin and a prick
It feels so serene
I love how it bleeds
My sweet necessity.

—Jeff West

THERE'S a Hole in My Sidewalk

I.

I walk down a street and there's a big hole.
I don't see it and fall into it.
It's dark and hopeless and it takes me a long time to find my
    way out.
It's not my fault!

II.

I walk down the same street.
There's a big hole and I can see it, but I still fall in.
It's dark and hopeless and it takes me a long time to get out.
It's still not my fault.

III.

I walk down a street.
There's a big hole.
I can see it, but I still fall in.
It's become a habit.
But I keep my eyes open and get out immediately.
It is my fault.

IV.

I walk down a street.
There's a big hole.
And I walk around it.

V.

I walk down a different street.

—Portia Nelson

D

How to Follow Your Soul's Guidance

1. Learn to **recognize your mind's chatter** and differentiate it from your soul's voice. If what is being said is fear-based, your human self's limiting conditioning is getting in the way.

2. **Develop a skill set to quiet your mind** based on your subjective experiences of what works. Customize this by using meditation, prayer, breath work, sound, and yoga, for example.

3. **State your intention** to connect with your soul. Do this on a regular basis until your connection deepens.

4. **Go into the silence** and really listen in order to hear the voice of your soul: your intuition.

5. Keep in the forefront that **your human self may not always like or want to hear** what your soul is saying/prompting you to do.

6. Become accustomed to **the qualitative difference of being connected with your soul** by experiencing energy (throughout your body) when your human self is connecting with your soul or a transmission is being made. Pause to feel the energy and receive what is being offered.

7. Tune into **the effect on your mind and your**

feeling state when your human self connects with your soul and works in unison.

8. Open your mind to *receive the prompting of your soul.* Your soul will instruct your human self what the next step is and inform you of which course of action to take.

9. *Your soul knows* what it has come into this lifetime to experience, along with each step to take in its unfolding process. Your soul will not lead your human self astray.

10. As your human self becomes more adept at reviewing your life, you will come to know that *when you listen to and follow your soul's guidance, the outcome is always favorable.*

11. Pay attention to *your mental conflicts.* If you want to become internally resourced, but are attempting to control a process or become attached to a particular outcome, you are saying one thing and doing another.

12. *Do not allow your mind to jump to conclusions* when your soul reveals something to your human self. Often times there is more information to follow. Keep an open mind.

13. Remember that *your soul is in the world to accomplish its mission,* leading to soul fulfillment. It is not here to be controlled or manipulated by societal dictates.

14. *Use caution* when acting on assumptions or presumptions. They are a clue that your human self

is in the driver's seat.

15. When in doubt about a decision or an action to take, *ask your soul for clarification, affirmation, or confirmation* on whatever you are in doubt or confused about.

16. *Learn to feel into your life.* Allow your body sensations to be factored into your decision-making processes.

17. *Stay present to your experience in the moment* in order to hear your intuition.

18. *Expect and normalize your fear* with the intention to transform it by aligning more fully with your soul.

19. Deepening in your relationship with your soul is *a lifelong endeavor*. Remember that practice makes better, and let go of the notion that your human self needs to do this perfectly.

20. Feeling *a deep abiding sense of serenity* is an indication that your human self is Living in Alignment with your soul.

21. Changing your perspective from being externally resourced to becoming internally resourced *increases your energy level*. Sustaining this energy requires deepening your awareness and staying connected to your soul.

22. Your human self will *require a lot of tender loving care*, especially in your initial experience of Living in Alignment. This courageous under-

taking usually brings up a lot of fear, including the fear of not getting your basic survival needs met, and also the fear of abandonment, betrayal, rejection, etc.

23. Living your life in a fear- or shame-based reality **impairs your ability to connect with your soul.** When this occurs you may tend to be over-identified with your 'story', preventing you from seeing how all your life circumstances are benefiting you.

24. The qualitative difference of **using your intuition** (the voice of your soul) to guide you relieves your mind, energizes your body, and offers your human self an increased sense of security, confidence, and deep abiding serenity.

25. Living in Alignment is about **listening to and following your soul's prompting.** With practice and persistence you can become proficient in determining when your soul is in the driver's seat rather than your human self. Strive to become increasingly aware of the qualitative difference between the two.

26. **Your soul will let your human self know** when you are not Living in Alignment by issuing wakeup calls that become more pronounced if you do not take heed.

27. You can develop your **awareness of the workings of your soul** by becoming more present. This involves accepting all aspects of your real-

ity. (You don't have to *like* what is happening.)

28. *When in doubt, don't.* Instead, wait for, listen to, and follow your soul's directives.

29. *Your soul communicates with your human self* in numerous ways: hunches, dreams, words spoken in your head, music, messages from other people, memories, thoughts, visions, perceptions, longings, synchronicities, body sensations, movies, observations about nature, ideas, emotions, art work, etc.

30. Remind yourself that *your soul always has the needs of your human self in the forefront* and advises you on the most effective ways to meet them.

THE Man in My Closet

There's a man in my closet
I think he controls me
    He's always around
    Can't see what he's doing
I open the doors
He sinks down deeper
    When he comes out
    A change in demeanor
The man in my closet
At times, he scares me
    He's done awful things
    Believes he is helping
Keep fixing the what
This somebody's done
    The man in my closet
    I wish he were gone
      —Jeff West

THROUGH the gateway of feeling your weakness
lies your strength;

Through the gateway of feeling your pain
lies your pleasure and joy;

Through the gateway of feeling your fear
lies your security and safety;

Through the gateway of feeling your loneliness
lies your capacity to have fulfillment, love, and
companionship;

Through the gateway of feeling your hate
lies your ability to love;

Through the gateway of feeling your hopelessness
lies true and justified hope;

Through the gateway of accepting the lacks in your
childhood
lies your fulfillment now.

—Eva Pierrakos

E

Professional Services to Sustain Your Recovery

HERE is a list of *practitioners and their main areas of focus* in working with people in recovery. Living in Alignment advocates the emerging perspective that *dependence is a symptom of underlying causes*. Until you identify and sufficiently address these, it is likely that substance abuse, addiction, and relapse will be ongoing life issues. You will want to work with a network of practitioners who embody a *'whole person'* approach to your recovery.

Acupuncturist: releases stored toxins in your body; stimulates and invigorates endorphin generation, works with reducing stress, food allergies, depression, anxiety, eating disorders, chronic fatigue, organ malfunction, gland malfunction, balances/promotes the natural flow of *qi* (vital energy); promotes internal cleansing and blood circulation; invigorates, regulates, and balances your mind, body, spirit.

Addiction specialist: clarifies and communicates the goals for each recovery stage; teaches relapse prevention skills; develops and implements aftercare planning; promotes 12-step and other support networks; ensures that you have appropriate structure and support.

Art therapist: facilitates release/expression of suppressed memories, emotions, integrating information from your subconscious mind.

Attorney: identifies and addresses legal issues affecting those in recovery as a result of consequences of their using behavior or choices and decisions made in recovery that require legal advice/appropriate action.

Body worker: improves overall circulation in your body; relieves stress; facilitates relaxation; works out tired, sore muscles; activates your body's natural healing processes; utilizes the healing qualities of touch, intuition, and the power of connection/release of trauma through your body.

Career counselor: conducts testing of aptitudes and interests, matching these with existing or future employment/career options, along with determining the best course of action to take to accomplish required schooling/desired goals.

Chiropractor: assists you to stay in physical/spinal alignment to foster optimal health of your nerves, muscles, and organs.

Dietitian/nutritionist: nutritional evaluation, dietary consultation/meal planning; addresses body image issues.

Hypnotherapist: facilitates the emergence of repressed memories, grounds/integrates internal shifts, and promotes healthy behaviors.

Life/spiritual coach: assists people to gain clarity to identify goals and implement lifestyle changes; work through unresolved religious/spiritual issues; develop a spiritual practice.

Medical doctor: detoxification and withdrawal; diagnosis of minor or major physical ailments; evaluates the functioning of glands and organs; conducts testing to determine if there are physiological/medical causes of chemical imbalances.

Naturopath: testing of neurotransmitters; conducts comprehensive blood panels; food allergy testing; determines deficiencies in key minerals and vitamins and provides supplements; prescribes and monitors various cleanses such as liver, gallbladder, colon, and blood.

Neurologist: conducts neurological tests to determine if existing nerve damage is causing physical pain/immobility.

Personal trainer: develops customized exercise programs to meet individual needs and goals that are appropriate to presenting conditions; teaches proper use of gym equipment; works through body image issues.

Psychiatrist: diagnosis of co-occurring mental disorders; evaluation, prescription, monitoring of pharmaceutical drugs.

Psychologist: diagnostic testing to determine physiological, cognitive, social functioning; cognitive behavioral therapy.

Psychotherapist: identifies and works through unresolved trauma-related issues, family of origin issues, dysfunctional thinking patterns, and coping behaviors; integrates new skills into behaviors; offers individual/couple/family counseling.

Yoga instructor: teaches poses to relieve mental/emotional/ physical stress and increase flexibility; integrates various meditation/visualization techniques to quiet and expand your mind.

RECOVERY
It isn't something you earn
It can't be bought in a store
It doesn't happen overnight
This you have to work for

It may take all your courage
It may take all your strength
It's a path you'll have to forge
If you want to live your life

There is no medication
There is no quick fix
Sometimes, in order to win
You have to put up a fight

You have to climb the mountain
You have to do what's right
You have to want it for yourself
There's no other way around it

A turning point in my recovery.

Understanding that the good things that were happening
and the happiness I was feeling were real;
That it came from me, only for me.
An inward realization of sorts:

O NLY Me
I gave it every chance to break
I tried so hard to make it fake

Maybe this time it is real
Maybe it's OK to feel

Maybe it is meant for me
The things that keep happening

Every time I've tried to touch it
Something came along to stop it

Every time that thing was fake
And now that I'm about to break

These things, they look very different
Humbled as I finally touch it

A very sentimental part
I treat it like a piece of art

Its only purpose is to be
For me to see and only me

—Jeff West

APPENDIX

F

Resources

12 Step

A Gentle Path through the Twelve Steps ~ Patrick Carnes, Ph.D.

A Woman's Way through the Twelve Steps ~ Stephanie S. Covington

Alcoholics Anonymous fact File: Traditions, 12 steps, and principles of Alcoholics Anonymous

The Twelve Steps and Dual Disorders ~ Tim Hamilton, Pat Samples

Twelve Steps and Twelve Traditions ~ Alcoholics Anonymous World Services

Abuse

Abused Boys: The Neglected Victims of Sexual Abuse ~ Mic Hunter

The Battered Women ~ Lonore E. Walker

The Courage To Heal: A Guide For Women Survivors of Sexual Abuse ~ Ellen Bass, Laura Davis

The Verbally Abusive Relationship: How To Recognize It and How To Respond ~ Patricia Evans

Victims No Longer: Men Recovering From Incest and Other Sexual Child Abuse ~ Mike Lew

Women Who Hurt Themselves ~ Dusty Miller

Alcohol/Drug Addiction

A Hole in the Sidewalk ~ Claudia Black, Ph.D.

Addiction-Free Pain Management: Relapse Prevention Counseling Workbook ~ Stephen F. Grinstead and Terence T. Gorski

Addictive Thinking: Understanding Self-Deception ~
    Abraham J. Twerski, M.D.
Adult Children of Alcoholics ~ Janet Geringer Woititz
*From Survival to Recovery: Growing Up in an Alcoholic
    Home* ~ Al-Anon Family Groups
Living Sober ~ Alcoholics Anonymous World Services
*Of Course You're Angry: A Guide to Dealing with the
    Emotions of Substance Abuse* ~ Gayle Rosellini, Mark
    Worden
Stepping Stones to Recovery: From Cocaine/Crack Addiction
    ~ Lisa D.
The Alcoholism & Addiction Cure ~ Pax & Chris Prentiss
The Courage to Change ~ Dennis Wholey
*Under The Influence: A Guide to the Myths and Realities of
    Alcoholism* ~ Dr. James R. Milam, Katherine Ketcham

Codependence

Beyond Codependency, and Getting Better All the Time ~
    Melody Beattie
*Dare To Be Yourself: How to Quit Being an Extra in Other
    People's Movies and Become the Star of Your Own* ~
    Alan Cohen
Do I Have to Give Up Me to be Loved by God? ~ Margaret
    Paul
Facing Codependence ~ Pia Melody
*Healing the Wounds of Codependence: a Guide to
    Reclaiming Your Life* ~ Darcy S. Clarke
Learning to Love Yourself: Finding Your Self Worth ~
    Sharon Wegscheider-Cruse
The Enabler: When Helping Harms The Ones You Love ~
    Angelyn Miller
The Language of Letting Go ~ Melody Beattie

Daily Meditations

A Cherokee Feast of Days: Daily Meditations ~ Joyce
    Sequichie Hifler
A Path with Heart ~ Jack Kornfield

A Woman's Spirit: More Meditations for Women ~ Karen Casey

Acts of Faith: Daily Meditations for People of Color ~ Iyanla Vanzant

Affirmations for the Inner Child ~ Rokelle Lerner

Answers in the Heart: Daily Meditations ~ Hazelden Meditation Series

Around the Year with Emmet Fox: A Book of Daily Readings ~ Emmet Fox

Believing in Myself: Daily Meditations for Healing and Building Self-Esteem ~ Earnie Larsen, Carol Hegarty

Daily Affirmations for Adult Children of Alcoholics ~ Rokelle Lerner

Each Day a New Beginning: Daily Meditations for Women ~ Karen Casey

Gathering Peace: A Journey of Discovery ~ Peggy Warren

Gentle Reminders: Daily Affirmations for Codependents ~ Mitzi Chandler

Glad Day: Daily Meditations For Gay, Lesbian, Bisexual & Transgender People ~ Joan Larkin

In God's Care: Daily Meditations on Spirituality in Recovery ~ Karen Casey

Journey to the Heart: Daily Meditations on the Path to Freeing Your Soul ~ Melody Beattie

Meditations for Men Who Do Too Much ~ Jonathon Lazear

Meditations for Women Who Do Too Much ~ Anne Wilson Schaef

Night Light: A Book of Nighttime Meditations ~ Amy E. Dean

Search for Serenity and How to Achieve It ~ Lewis F. Presnall

Touchstones: A Book of Daily Meditations for Men ~ Hazelden Foundation

Yesterday's Tomorrow: Recovery Meditations For Hard Cases ~ Barry L.

Diagnostic and Treatment Issues

Over Diagnosed: Making People Sick in the Pursuit of Health ~ H. Gilbert Welch, M.D., Lisa M. Schwartz, M.D., Steve Woloshin, M.D.

Overdosed America: The Broken Promise of American Medicine ~ John Abramson, M.D.

Prescription for Drug Alternatives: All Natural Options for Better Health without the Side Effects ~ James Balch, M.D., Mark Stengler, N.D., Robin Young Balch, N.D.

Selling Sickness: How the World's Biggest Pharmaceutical Companies Are Turning Us All into Patients ~ Ray Moynihan, Alan Cassels

The Truth About the Drug Companies: How They Deceive Us and What to Do About It ~ Marcia Angel

Emotions

A Journey Through Grief ~ Alla Renée Bozarth, Ph.D.

A Path with Heart ~ Jack Kornfield

Feel the Fear and Do It Anyway ~ Susan Jeffers, Ph.D.

Feelings Buried Alive Never Die ~ Karol K. Truman

Gathering Peace: A Journey of Discovery ~ Peggy Warren

I Don't Want to Talk About It ~ Terry Real

Love Is Letting Go of Fear ~ Gerald G. Jampolsky, M.D.

Molecules of Emotion ~ Candace B. Pert, Ph.D.

Of Course You're Angry: A Guide to Dealing with the Emotions of Substance Abuse ~ Gayle Rosellini, Mark Worden

Shame and Guilt: The Masters of Disguise ~ Jane Middelton-Moz

The Creative Journal: The Art of Finding Yourself ~ Lucia Capacchione

The Intimacy Factor ~ Pia Mellody, Lawrence S. Freundlich

The Anger Workbook ~ Loraine Bilodeau, M.S.

Your Body Is Your Subconscious Mind ~ Candace Pert, Ph.D.

Family Issues

Adult Children: The Secrets of Dysfunctional Families ~
 John Friel, Linda Friel
Always Daddy's Girl ~ H. Norman Wright
Before You Forget ~ Kelly DuMar
Children of Trauma: Rediscovering Your Discarded Self ~
 Jane Middelton-Moz
Coming Out: An Act of Love ~ Rob Eichberg, Ph.D.
Facing Shame ~ Merle A Fossum, Marilyn Mason
Family Secrets: The Path to Self Acceptance and Reunion ~
 John Bradshaw
Freeing Our Families from Perfection ~ Thomas S.
 Greenspon, Ph.D.
*Growing Up Again: Parenting Ourselves, Parenting Our
 Children* ~ Jean Illsley Clarke, Connie Dawson
How to Talk so Kids Will Listen & Listen so Kids will Talk ~
 Adele Faber, Elaine Mazlish
Longing For Dad: Father Loss and its Impact ~ Beth M.
 Erickson, Ph.D.
Love You Forever ~ Robert Munsch
My Mother, My Self: The Daughter's Search for Self ~ Nancy
 Friday
Self Esteem: A Family Affair ~ Jean Illsely Clarke
Shame And Guilt: The Masters of Disguise ~ Jane
 Middelton-Moz
Silently Seduced: When Parents Make Children Partners ~
 Kenneth M Adams, Ph.D.
The Birth Order Book ~ Dr. Kevin Leman
The Drama of the Gifted Child ~ Alice Miller
The Emotional Incest Syndrome ~ Dr. Patricia Love
The Worst Loss ~ Barbara D. Rosof

Inspiration

A Journey Through Grief ~ Alla Renée Bozarth, Ph.D.
*Be Who You Want, Have What You Want: change your
 thinking, change your life* ~ Chris Prentiss

Gathering Peace: A Journey of Discovery ~ Peggy Warren
Kitchen Table Wisdom: Stories That Heal ~ Rachel Naomi
   Remen, M.D.
One Day My Soul Just Opened Up ~ Iyanla Vanzant
The Giving Tree ~ Shel Silverstein
The Healing Drum ~ Blackwolf Jones, Gina Jones
When Bad Things Happen to Good People ~ Harold Kushner
Why Your Life Sucks and What You Can Do About It ~ Alan
   H. Cohen
Zen and the Art of Happiness ~ Chris Prentiss

Love Addiction

Facing Love Addiction ~ Pia Mellody
Leaving The Enchanted Forest ~ Stephanine Covington,
   Liana Beckett
Women, Sex and Addiction ~ Charlotte Davis Kasl, Ph.D.

Mood Disorders

An Unquiet Mind: a Memoir of Moods and Madness ~ Kay
   Redfield Jamison, Ph.D.
Manic: a Memoir ~ Terri Cheney
*Mind Over Mood: Change How You Feel by Changing the
   Way You Think* ~ Dennis Greenberger, PhD, Christine A.
   Padesky, Ph.D.
*The Bipolar Disorder Survival Guide: What You and Your
   Family Need to Know* ~ David J. Miklowitz, Ph.D.
*The Up and Down Life: the Truth About Bipolar Disorder—
   the Good, the Bad, and the Funny* ~ Paul E. Jones
To Walk on Eggshells ~ Jean Johnson
Wishful Drinking ~ Carrie Fisher

Other Addictions

*Chained to the Desk: A Guidebook for Workaholics, Their
   Partners and Children, and the Clinicians Who Treat
   Them* ~ Bryan E. Robinson
*How to Get Out of Debt, Stay Out of Debt, and Live
   Prosperously* ~ Jerrold Mundis

Money Drunk, Money Sober: 90 Days To Financial Freedom
~ Julia Cameron, Mark Bryan
Too Perfect: When Being in Control Gets Out of Control ~
Allan E. Mallinger, M.D., Jeannette DeWyze
*Working Ourselves to Death: The High Cost of Workaholism
and the Rewards of Recovery* ~ Diane Fassel

Recovery

*Accepting Ourselves and Others: A Journey into Recovery
from Addictive and Compulsive Behaviors for Gays,
Lesbians and Bisexuals* ~ Sheppard B. Kominars, Ph.D.,
Kathryn D. Kominars, Ph.D.
Addiction and Grace ~ Gerald G. May, M.D.
Changing Course ~ Claudia Black, Ph.D.
Coming Out Of Shame: Transforming Gay and Lesbian Lives
~ Gershen Kaufman, Ph.D., Lev Raphael. Ph.D.
Disclosing Secrets ~ Jennifer Schneider, Debra Corley
Good Grief ~ Ganger E. Westberg
It's Never too Late to Have a Happy Childhood ~ Claudia
Black, Ph.D.
*Letting Go of Shame: Understanding How Shame Affects
Your Life* ~ Ronald Potter-Efron, Patricia Potter-Efron
Recovery Equation ~ Pavel Somov
Self Esteem: A Family Affair ~ Jean Isely Clarke
Taking Responsibility ~ Nathaniel Branden, Ph.D.
The Creative Journal: The Art of Finding Yourself ~ Lucia
Capacchione
The Power of Two: Secrets to a Strong and Loving Marriage
~ Susan Heitler, Ph.D.
The Primal Wound: Understanding the Adopted Child ~
Nancy Newton Verrier
Today I Feel Silly and Other Moods that Make My Day ~
Jamie Lee Curtis
Twelve Jewish Steps to Recovery ~ Rabbi Kerry M. Olitzky
and Stuart A. Copans, M.D.
Workaholics: The Respectable Addicts ~ Barbara Killinger,
Ph.D.

Relationships

After the Affair: Healing the Pain and Rebuilding Trust When a Partner Has Been Unfaithful ~ Janis Abrahms Spring, Ph.D.

Awakening Your Sexuality: A Guide for Recovering Women ~ Stephanie S. Covington, Ph.D.

Boundaries and Relationships ~ Charles L. Whitfield, M.D.

Getting Love Right: Learning the Choices of Healthy Intimacy ~ Terence T. Gorski

Getting the Love You Want ~ Harville Hendrix, Ph.D.

Heartwounds: The Impact of Unresolved Trauma and Grief on Relationships ~ Tian Dayton, Ph.D.

How Can I get Through to You ~ Terrence Real

I Love You Enough to Let You Go ~ Jim McGregor

If Only He Knew: Understanding Your Wife ~ Gary Smalley

The Dance of Intimacy: A Woman's Guide to Courageous Acts of Change in Key Relationships ~ Harriet Lerner, Ph.D.

The Knight in Rusty Armor ~ Robert Fisher

Undefended Love ~ Jett Psaris and Marlena Tyons

Why Am I Afraid to Love ~ John Powell, S.J.

You Just Don't Understand: Women and Men in Conversation ~ Deborah Tannen, Ph.D.

Sex Addiction

Cybersex Unhooked: A Workbook for Breaking Free of Compulsive Online Sexual Behavior ~ David L. Delmonico, Ph.D., Elizabeth Griffin, Joseph Moriarity

Facing The Shadow ~ Patrick Carnes, Ph.D.

In the Shadows of the Net: Breaking Free of Complusive Online Sexual Behavior ~ Patrick Carnes, David Delmonico, Elizabeth Griffin

No Stones ~ Marnie C. Ferree

Open Hearts: Renewing Relationships with Recovery, Romance & Reality ~ Patrick Carnes, Ph.D.

Sexual Anorexia: Overcoming Sexual Self-Hatred ~ Patrick Carnes, Ph.D. with Joseph M. Moriarity

Spirituality

A Return to Love ~ Marianne Williamson
Addiction and Grace ~ Gerald G. May, M.D.
Awakening: Conversations with the Master ~ Anthony de Mello
Awareness: The Perils and Opportunities of Reality ~ Anthony de Mello
Discover Your Soul Connection ~ Darcy S. Clarke
Earth Dance Drum: A Celebration of Life ~ Blackwolf Jones, Gina Jones
Experience Living in Alignment: A Practical Guide to Personal Transformation ~ Darcy S. Clarke
Finding Your Way Home ~ Melody Beattie
Illuminata: A Return to Prayer ~ Marianne Williamson
Let Me Grieve But Not Forever ~ Verdell Davis
Living in Process: Basic Truths for Living the Path ~ Anne Wilson Schaef
Practicing the Power of Now ~ Eckhart Tolle
Rising to the Call ~ Jacquelyn Small and Mary Yovino
Seven Arrows ~ Hyemeyohsts Storm
Soul Mission, Life Vision ~ Alan Seale
The Four Agreements ~ Don Miguel Ruiz
The Hero with a Thousand Faces ~ Joseph Campbell
The Inner Voice ~ Henri J. M. Nouwen
The Leader as Martial Artist ~ Arnold Mindell
The Warrior's Journey Home: Healing Men, Healing the Planet ~ Jed Diamond

Stress and Anxiety Disorders

Anxiety 101: The Holistic Approach to Managing Your Anxiety & Taking Back Your Life ~ Eudene Harry, M.D.
Controlling Stress and Tension ~ Daniel A. Girdano, Dorothy E. Dusek, George S. Everly, Jr.

Managing Stress: Principles and Strategies for Health and Well-Being ~ Brian Luke Seaward

Freedom from Anxiety: A Holistic Approach to Emotional Well-Being ~ Marcy Shapiro, M.D., Barbara L. Vivino Ph.D.

Peace of Mind: Holistic Approaches to Anxiety and ADD ~ Ronald R. Parks, M.D.

The Mood Cure: the 4-Step Program to Take Charge of Your Emotions-Today ~ Julia Ross

Recovery Organizations

Adult Children of Alcoholics (**ACA**) World Services 562-595-7831 www.adultchildren.org

Al-Anon/Alateen Family Group Headquarters 757/563-1600 www.al-anon.alateen.org

Alcoholics Anonymous (**AA**) World Services 212/870-3400 www.aa.org

Celebrate Recovery www.celebraterecovery.com

Co-Dependents Anonymous (**CoDA**) 602/277-7991 coda.org

Cocaine Anonymous (**CA**) World Services 310/559-5833 www.ca.org

Crystal Meth Anonymous (**CMA**) 855/638-4373 www.crystalmeth.org

Gamblers Anonymous® (**GA**) 626/960-3500 www.gamblersanonymous.org

LifeRing Secular Recovery 800/811-4142 www.lifering.org

Marijuana Anonymous (**MA**) World Services 800/766-6779 www.marijuana-anonymous.org

Narcotics Anonymous (**NA**) World Services 818/773-9999 www.na.org

Overeaters Anonymous, Inc.® (**OA**) 505/891-2664 www.oa.org

Pills Anonymous (**PA**) World Services 800/321-2211 www.pillsanonymous.org

Rational Recovery® 530/621-2667 www.rational.org

Secular Organizations for Sobriety (**SOS**)
  323/666-4295 www.sossobriety.org
Sex Addicts Anonymous (**SAA**)
  800/477-8191 https://saa-recovery.org
SMART Recovery®
  866/951-5357 www.smartrecovery.org
Women For Sobriety, Inc.
  215/536-8026 www.womenforsobriety.org
Workaholics Anonymous
  510/273-9253 www.workaholics-anonymous.org

Referral Sources

National Suicide Prevention Lifeline 800/273-TALK (8255)
Treatment Referral Line
  800/662-HELP (4357) http://findtreatment.samhsa.gov/
Find a doctor: www.freemedicalsearch.org/
Find a therapist, psychiatrist, therapy group, or treatment
  center: www.PsychologyToday.com

Other Resources

Sounds True catalogue of self-help on holistic approaches to
  health and well being, CD, MP downloads
  800/333-9185 SoundsTrue.com

Centers

Kripalu Center for Yoga & Health 800/741-7853 kripalu.org
Omega Institute for Holistic Studies/Rhinebeck NY
  877/944-2002 www.eomega.org

Video

For a more complete list of movies related to alcohol/drug
addiction, google *Addiction and Recovery Film Series*.

28 Days 2000; 103 mins.
A big-city newspaper columnist is forced to enter a drug
and alcohol rehab center after ruining her sister's wedding
and crashing a stolen limousine.
Director: Betty Thomas; Stars: Sandra Bullock, Viggo
Mortensen

Another Day in Paradise 1998; 101 mins.
In the hope of a big score, two junkie couples team up to commit various drug robberies that go disastrously wrong leading to dissent, violence, and murder.
Director: Larry Clark; Stars: James Woods, Melanie Griffith, Vincent Kartheiser

The Basketball Diaries 1995; 102 mins.
Film adaptation of Street tough Jim Carroll's epistle about his kaleidoscopic free fall into the harrowing world of drug addiction.
Director: Scott Kalvert; Stars: Leonardo DiCaprio

Crazy Heart 2009; 112 mins.
A faded country music musician is forced to reassess his dysfunctional life during a doomed romance that also inspires him.
Director: Scott Cooper; Stars: Jeff Bridges, Maggie Gyllenhaal, Colin Farrell

Down to the Bone 2004; 104 mins.
A woman stuck in a stale marriage struggles to raise her children and manage her secret drug habit. But when winter comes to her small town, her balancing act begins to come crashing down.
Director: Debra Granik; Stars: Vera Farmiga, Hugh Dillon, Clint Jordan

Drugstore Cowboy 1989; 102 mins.
A realistic road movie about a drug addict, his 'family', and their inevitable decline into crime.
Director: Gus Van Sant Jr.; Stars: Matt Dillon, Kelly Lynch, James LeGros

Changing Lanes 2002; 98 mins.
The story of what happens one day in New York when a young lawyer and a businessman share a small automobile accident on FDR Drive and their mutual road rage escalates into a feud.

Director: Roger Michell; Stars: Ben Affleck, Samuel L. Jackson, Toni Collette

Clean and Sober 1998; 124 mins.
A hustling drug addict checks himself into rehab to escape trouble with the law, and realizes that it's exactly what he needs.
Director: Glenn Gordon Caron; Stars: Michael Keaton, Morgan Freeman

Everything Must Go 2010; 97 mins.
When an alcoholic relapses, causing him to lose his wife and his job, he holds a yard sale on his front lawn in an attempt to start over. A new neighbor might be the key to his return ort form.
Director: Dan Rush; Stars: Will Ferrell, Christopher Jordan Wallace

Gia 1998; 120 mins.
The life of Gia Carangi, a top fashion model in the late 70's, from her meteoric rise to the forefront of the modeling industry, to her untimely death from AIDS at age 26.
Director: Michael Cristofer; Stars: Angelina Jolie, Faye Dunaway

Gridlock'd 1997; 91 mins.
After a friend overdoses, Spoon and Stretch decide to kick their drug habits and attempt to enroll in a government detox program.
Director: Vondie Curtis-Hall; Stars: Tupac Shakur, Tim Ruth, Thandie Newton

I Am a Sex Addict 2005; 98 mins.
Autobiographical comedy about a recovering sex addict, about his obsession with prostitutes, and how that affected his relationships and his life altogether.
Director: Caveh Zahedi; Stars: Caveh Zahedi, Christoff Colas, Rebecca Lord

I'm Dancing as Fast as I Can 1982; 107 mins.
A true story about Emmy-winning documentary filmmaker Barbara Gordon's Valium addiction and her desperate attempts to kick the habit.
Director: Jack Hofsiss; Stars: Jill Clayburgh, Dianne Wiest, Joe Pesci

Jesus' Son 1999; 107 mins.
A young man turns from drug addiction and petty crime to a life redeemed by a discovery of compassion.
Director: Alison Maclean; Stars: Billy Crudup, Robert Michael Kelly

Leaving Las Vegas 1995; 111 mins.
Ben Sanderson, an alcoholic Hollywood screenwriter who lost everything because of his drinking, arrives in Vegas to drink himself to death. There he meets and forms an uneasy friendship and non-interference pact with prostitute Sera.
Director: Mike Figgis; Stars: Nicolas Cage, Elisabeth Shue, Julian Sands

Less Than Zero 1987; 98 mins.
A college freshman returns to L.A. for the holidays at his ex-girlfriend's request, but discovers that his former best friend has an out-of-control drug habit.
Director: Marek Kanievska; Stars: Robert Downey Jr, James Spader

The Lost Weekend 1945; 101 mins.
The desperate life of a chronic alcoholic followed through a 4 day drinking bout.
Director: Billy Wilder; Stars: Ray Milland, Jane Wyman, Howard Da Silva

The Man with the Golden Arm 1955; 119 mins.
A strung-out junkie deals with daily demoralizing drug addiction while crippled wife and card sharks continue to pull him down.
Director: Otto Preminger; Stars: Frank Sinatra, Kim Novak

My Name Is Bill W. 1989; 100 mins.
Based on the true story of AA founder Bill W., a successful stockbroker whose life falls apart after the 1929 crash.
Director: Daniel Petrie; Stars: James Woods, James Garner, Gary Sinise

My Own Private Idaho 1991; 104 mins.
Two best friends living on the streets of Portland as hustlers embark on a journey of self discovery and find their relationship stumbling along the way.
Director: Gus van Sant; Stars: River Phoenix, Keanu Reeves, James Russo

Once Were Warriors 1994; 102 mins.
A family descended from Maori warriors is bedeviled by a violent father and problems of being treated as outcasts.
Director: Lee Tamahori; Stars: Rena Owen, Temuera Morrison

Postcards from the Edge 1990; 101 mins.
Substance-addicted Hollywood actress Suzanne Vale is on the skids. After detox her company insists as a condition of working that she live with her domineering mother, once a star and now a champion drinker. Bitingly funny!
Director: Mike Nichols; Stars: Meryl Streep, Shirley Maclaine, Dennis Quaid

Rachel Getting Married 2008; 113 mins.
A young woman who has been in and out from rehab for the past 10 years returns home for the weekend for her sister's wedding.
Director: Jonathan Demme; Stars: Anne Hathaway, Rosemarie DeWitt

Requiem for a Dream 2000; 102 mins.
The drug-induced utopias of four Coney Island people are shattered when their addictions become stronger.
Director: Darren Aronofsky; Stars: Ellen Burstyn, Jared Leto, Jennifer Connelly

Sid and Nancy (1986; 112 mins.
Morbid biographical story of Sid Vicious, bassist with British punk group the Sex Pistols, and his girlfriend Nancy Spungen.
Director: Alex Cox; Stars: Gary Oldman, Chloe Webb, David Hayman

Rush 1991; 120 mins.
Two small town Texas cops go undercover to catch a major drug dealer and are sucked into the drug culture, compromising their assignment.
Director: Lili Fini Zanuck; Stars: Jason Patric, Jennifer Jason Leigh, Sam Elliott

Spun 2002; 101 mins.
An out-of-control speed freak is introduced his drug of choice's creator by his dealer. A massive three-day adventure ensues.
Director: Jonas Akerlund; Stars: Jason Schwartzman, John Leguizamo

Stuart Saves His Family 1995; 95 mins.
A self-help advocate struggles to put his dysfunctional family in its place.
Director: Harold Ramis; Stars: Al Franken, Laura San Giacomo

Things We Lost in the Fire 2007; 118 mins.
A recent widow invites her husband's troubled best friend to live with her and her two children. As he gradually turns his life around, he helps the family confront their loss.
Director: Susanne Bier; Stars: Halle Berry, Benicio Del Toro, David Duchovny

Unguarded 2011; 90 mins.
Chris Herren was a "can't miss" basketball superstar until drug addiction eventually destroyed his career. With the support of his wife and family, Herren struggles to conquer his demons and reclaim his life.

Director: Jonathan Hock; Stars: Chris Herren, Rick Pitino, Bill Reynolds

When a Man Loves a Woman 1994; 126 mins.
An airline pilot and his wife are forced to face the consequences of her alcoholism when her addictions threaten her life and their daughter's safety. While the woman enters detox, her husband must face the truth of his enabling behavior.
Director: Luis Mandok; Stars: Meg Ryan, Andy Garcia, Ellen Burstyn

THERE is no God independent of us.
Source energy is outside and inside us,
it is omnipresent,
it is consciousness itself!

If you are a seeker after truth,
you will come to realize
that your intellect alone
is powerless to transform your life.

Choose this insight as the springboard
for your human self to merge
with the transforming energy
of higher consciousness.

DEEP Inside
Standing on the beach
Sand between my toes,
What lies of the future?
Who will come and go?

The sun beams down upon me
As I raise my head and look
At the vast ocean before me
Its size which I mistook

I feel so insignificant
Compared to its expanse
What difference could I make?
Will I even be given a chance?

I realized then while standing there
That all I have to do
Is listen to my heart
And it will pull me through.

For strength and inspiration
Are not material things
They come from deep inside of you
They give your soul its wings

So whenever you're in doubt
And you begin to stray
Listen to your soul
And the answer will come your way.

If only you believe in you
It can make your dreams come true
For no one else can do it
The power must come from you.

—Arielle Perkins

G

Glossary
Terms used in the Living in Alignment Model

AUTHENTICITY: Fully accepting that you are *both human and spiritual*. Being authentic is living in your truth and being empowered: owning your mental, emotional, physical, spiritual, and behavioral reality. It is knowing that being genuinely *real* with yourself and others in all of your relations is *the best gift* you can offer. Your authenticity is an invitation for others to be authentic.

BEHAVIORAL addictions: Activities like compulsive sex, eating, gambling, spending, work, internet use, and exercising are classified as *process* addictions. Drug and alcohol addictions are classified as *substance* addictions, resulting in physiological and psychological *dependence*. The difference lies in what you are addicted to. With a behavioral addiction, you become addicted to the *process* or *procedure* involved in the activity.

Boundaries: Limits you place on yourself and others. They are to be established and maintained as a means to *protect* yourself from others, *protect* others from yourself, and *protect* yourself from harmful/abusive conduct or thinking.

CONDITIONS: The mental, emotional, physical, sexual, and spiritual *energy patterns* everyone has. They are not *who* you are. Understanding and accepting your conditions will increase your awareness of how Source energy is working in your life. How you *relate* to these energy patterns will determine whether they keep you hostage (in *'victim consciousness'*) or hasten your process of transformation (achieving your full potential).

Consciousness: Source energy, Higher Power, God, Buddha Mind, the Divine, and all other names used to refer to the underlying *essence* of all things seen and unseen. To have a conscious living experience is to be aware that we are all *manifestations* of consciousness itself.

Co-occurring Disorders: A *dual diagnosis* with substance use and a co-existing mental disorder that results from an existing biological or medical condition or is induced and/or exacerbated by substance use. Many people with a substance use disorder began using in an attempt to *self-medicate* an existing mental/physical condition.

EGO: A product of your conditioning, this aspect of your mind perceives yourself as *separate* and is primarily preoccupied with your human needs and wants: *survival* and the pursuit of *pleasure*. If unchecked, this perception develops into self-centeredness and *narcissism*. Once your human self starts Living in Alignment with your soul, you will experience more security and love and increase your ability to listen to and follow the guidance and prompting of your soul's voice (your intuition).

Emotion: The energetic *charge* of feelings in motion, flowing through you. Your emotions offer you valuable information about what is happening in both your internal (mind/body) and external reality, as well as insights from your soul.

Emotional Presence: The quality of being able to identify, feel, and appropriately share your *feelings* with yourself and others.

Energy: The essence of what everything is made of. Energy is the source of consciousness. Everyone experiences different energy levels. You can learn to *regulate* your energy, *partner* with Source energy, and become conscious of how you are *co-creating* your reality with your thoughts, perceptions, behaviors, expectations, beliefs, attitudes, and intentions.

Energy 'Block': Energy that gets stuck due to the restriction or *constriction* of Source energy. You may be aware that 'something' is *blocking* you from moving forward in your life with clarity and purpose, but you may not have a clue about what you are habitually feeling and/or doing that is creating or perpetuating your 'blocked' energy.

Energy 'Leak': An experience of Source energy (vitality) that is being psychologically and emotionally *dissipated* to a greater or lesser extent on an ongoing basis. As with energy 'blocks', you may be aware that your energy level is *down*, but may not have a clue as to what is causing this depletion.

Externally resourced: Allowing *outside influences* to rule you. This plays out in all aspects of your life, including the profession you choose, if and whom you marry, how and where you worship, where you live, what make of car you drive, whom you associate with, etc. When you are externally resourced, you will live in fear because your connection to Source energy is minimal and/or not integrated.

FORGIVENESS: The act of *releasing* someone (or yourself) from a 'mistake' or wrongdoing. Forgiving does not mean forgetting what happened but rather making the choice to let go of *resentment* and preoccupation with *transgressions*. Identifying and integrating the insights being offered are effective methods of helping your mind release its grip.

GROUNDEDNESS: A secure, felt sense of being present in the moment *and in touch* with all aspects of your reality: your thoughts, emotions, intuitions, sensations, and experiences of living in your body and taking care of your earthly responsibilities and your soul's needs.

HEALTHY Shame is a common feeling when you are seen making a *mistake*. You feel exposed and embarrassed, become aware of your human limitations, hold yourself accountable, and change your behavior.

Higher Power: The *Source* of everything that is, was, and shall be. A benevolent, interactive, ingenious, creative, and unifying *energy system*, this higher Power is constantly *evolving* as well as beyond our mental comprehension.

Humanness: Your *integration* of your physical body, your intellect, your personality and emotions, and your soul.

INTEGRATION: Living in your truth, 'walking your talk' in your daily life, and *connecting* your mind/body with your soul. Your journey from your head to your heart is about *integrating* the insights, gifts, and lessons available within your life experiences.

Internally resourced: Taking outside influences into account, but primarily tuning into your *inner self* to access and follow the directives of your soul.

LAPSE (or Slip): Ending a period of abstinence by *resuming* your using behaviors, but being able to stop using before the substance gains complete power and control over your mind and body.

Living in Alignment: The *awakening* process in which your human self/personality *connects* with your soul. As this happens you ensure that your soul will complete its mission by following its directives. Thus your human self accepts its rightful position as the agent of your soul.

PSYCHOACTIVE or PSYCHOTROPIC drugs: Substances that act primarily on the Central Nervous System, affecting brain functioning (the levels of neurotransmitters in the brain), and resulting in *alterations* of perception, mood, consciousness, cognitions, and behavior.

REALITY: In conscious or unconscious *partnership* with Source energy, you *co-create* your reality and are intended to *accept* your sensations, perceptions, intuitions, beliefs, emotions, attitudes, thoughts, expectations, **intentions, conditions, behaviors, and experiences of living** in your body and meeting both your human needs and your soul needs.

Recovery: In the context of the Living in Alignment Model, recovery refers to the process of *reclaiming* your personal power (or connection with Source energy) you have *given away* to addictions, other people, conditions, events, and/or limiting conditioning.

Relapse: Resuming your pattern of using alcohol or other addictive substances after a period of abstinence. Refers to both substance *abuse* and substance *dependence* that reactivates your brain's reward center.

Religion: Refers to individual beliefs and opinions concerning the existence, nature, and/or worship of a deity or deities. The operative word here is 'belief', as opposed to 'knowing' from direct experience. Oftentimes those who are 'religious' think that they need an *intermediary* to connect with a higher Power. In addition, those who are 'religious' tend to *give their power away* to an outside authority and/or get caught up in *dogma*.

SEEN REALITY: The three-dimensional external world that is *perceived* by your five senses.

Shame-based reality: When you become identified with your shame, you experience yourself as *inferior* (taking a one-up or one-down position with others), as well as seeing yourself as *defective* and your life as *worthless*. Shame-based reality *results* from not being fully acknowledged as a unique reflection of Source energy; being taught that you are a *sinner* and that your life is about repenting; having experienced traumatic events and interpreting these events from a place of *blaming* and holding yourself responsible; years of self-deprecation; living with people who are shaming.

Soul: Who you are in your deepest nature. Your soul is your *essence*. Each soul is a unique aspect and reflection of Source energy. It continues to exist after your body dies.

Soul actualization: Living up to your full potential in this lifetime and engaging in your *soul mission*.

Soul fulfillment: Your experience of deep and abiding joy, happiness, and peace as you *manifest* your life calling.

Soul mission: What your soul yearns to realize in this world: your *freedom to be* fully human, to manifest your *unique* potential, and to *engage* with passion the particular circumstances you have co-created with Source energy.

Soul realization: Occurs when you both recognize and acknowledge that on the deepest level of your being, you are a living, breathing aspect of Source energy (your soul) manifested in your physical body. It is knowing that all life forms are manifestations of Source energy, that *We are all ONE*. It is knowing that your presence in your physical body living on Planet Earth is significant and that your life has meaning and purpose.

Source energy: A benevolent, interactive, ingenious, creative, omnipresent, unifying, and self-generating energy system, Source energy is in a constant state of *evolution* as well as *beyond* our mental comprehension. It is the wellspring of everything that is, was, and shall be.

Spiritual awakening: Developing your intuitive *awareness* that you are *both* a spiritual being *and* a human being living in your physical body. You are a *unique* reflection of, and have direct access to Source energy. The unseen world of *mystery* is as real as what you see. All life forms are *sacred*, *interconnected*, and *interdependent*. Your life has meaning and purpose and is important in the *evolution* of consciousness itself.

Spiritual bypassing: *Avoiding* certain aspects of your earthly existence by *focusing* on spiritual beliefs and practices and *denying* the importance of your earthly experiences. This can take the form of 'meditating' away your uncomfortable feelings, living in *denial*, minimizing aspects of your reality, *not* taking responsibility for your life, *not* holding yourself accountable for your decisions and choices, *not* taking care of your basic needs or *expecting* others or Source energy to do it for you, leading your life from a place of *entitlement*, etc.

Story, Your: The *rigid ideas you construct* around the events you experience (past and present). When you are *stuck* in your story, you become *fixated* on the *literal* interpretation of what is happening in your life (what you make out to be the facts). In other words, you may find yourself getting *stuck* in your cognitions. Subsequently, drama ensues in terms of who is to *blame* and who is right; *resentments* build, nothing gets resolved, and you stay focused on your problem.

Substance Abuse: A *maladaptive* pattern of substance use leading to clinically significant impairment or distress, manifesting in one or more of the following: recurrent substance use resulting in failure to fulfill major role obligations at work, school, or home; recurrent substance use that is physically hazardous; recurrent substance-related legal problems; continued substance use despite having persistent or recurrent social or interpersonal problems caused or exacerbated by the effects of the substance.

Substance Addiction: Something you *have*, not who you *are*. As with all conditions (mental, emotional, physical) if viewed from your soul's perspective, addictions can be used for the purpose of *transformation*. Addiction is a *strategy* your human self *chooses* to try to control (cope with) life challenges. The disease model defines substance addiction as being characterized by an inability to abstain consistently, impairment in behavioral control, craving, diminished recognition of significant problems with one's behaviors and interpersonal relationships, and a dysfunctional emotional response. Like other chronic diseases, addiction often involves *cycles of relapse and remission*. Without treatment or engagement in recovery activities, addiction is *progressive* and can result in disability or premature death.

Substance Dependence: physiological and/or psychological *impairment* or *distress* resulting from chronic substance use that produces *craving*/compulsive seeking, a *rush*/high/brain reward, *tolerance*/increased use/decreased effects, inability to cut back or *stop*, and *withdrawal* syndromes after stopping abruptly ('going cold turkey'), including palpitations, fever, hypertension, confusion, fatigue, irritability, anxiety, nausea, diarrhea, sweating, shivering, shaking (DT's), vomiting, convulsions, seizures, tremors, agitation, disorientation, depression, insomnia, headache/severe physical pain, panic attacks, hallucinations, psychosis, and rebound symptoms that may be relieved by using a psychoactive substance.

Sustainable Transformation: A lifelong process of integrating insights, gifts, and lessons from your soul's interaction with your human self that *sustains an internal shift* in your awareness: focusing on your life calling and allowing you to accomplish it in the context of your life circumstances while also meeting your human needs.

Synchronicity: An energetic phenomenon (a seeming coincidence) that occurs when you are asking for and aligning with the greatest potential of *what wants to happen* in any given moment or situation. You can view it as a confirmation that something of *importance* is occurring. This may take many forms, such as a person coming into your life at a crucial time; a new opportunity; a solution to a problem, etc.

TOXIC Shame: A feeling that results from believing that *I am bad, something is wrong with me, I am not OK, I am not lovable, I am not enough.* It is a combination of dishonor and feeling defective, undeserving, and unworthy. You are not born with toxic shame. It is *the result of your conditioning*: not being seen and respected as a spiritual/human being; internalizing shaming messages; and taking on other people's shame.

Triggers are reactions to situations or emotional states that activate your sympathetic nervous system (fight/flight) responses. Their *overwhelming* intensity makes it difficult to remain *present* to using stimuli, stressful or traumatic experiences, and flashbacks. Applying effective coping skills offers opportunities to *deepen* in your recovery. Inadequate coping skills are likely to lead to *relapse*.

UNITY CONSCIOUSNESS: Your embodied experience of connecting with Source energy or consciousness itself, *being at One* with all creation, and *transcending polarizing perspectives* (right/wrong, good/bad, sexual/spiritual, mind/body, self/other, winner/loser, human/divine).

Unseen Reality: The real world you can experience through your *intuition* but cannot perceive with your five senses. It is both within and beyond your three-dimensional reality.

OUT of Time
44 years have taken their toll
A constant struggle, I feel so old

Nothing has changed in all of those years
A life lived for others to keep away fears

All of the drinking to try and fit in
All of the drugs that made me so thin

So tired of this I've had enough
Disgusted of what I have become

Exhausted from my own façade
Praying that there is a God

Take the one thing that is mine
But how to leave my kids behind

Don't want to wreck their precious souls
Seems so cruel to miss them grow

There is no way to fix my mind
I'm sadly running out of time
—Jeff West

Index of Poetry
By Title or First Line

By Author

Acknowledgements

I **OFFER** gratitude to all the people I have worked with over the years: those who have placed their trust in me as a catalyst for their healing and transformative processes. They have been my teachers, and their lives have been laboratories in assisting me to develop this material into its current manifestation.

I offer gratitude to the people who have contributed poetry. Their words convey the depth of their experiences, their struggles, and their longing to reclaim their power and their lives from substance abuse/dependence and other conditions, people, events, traumas, limiting beliefs and ways of thinking, etc.

I offer gratitude to the many people in the recovery field who have influenced my work over the years, including Jacqueline Small, Gabor Mate, Chris Prentiss, Claudia Black, Patrick Carnes, Melody Beattie, Caroline Myss, Pia Mellody, and many others.

I offer gratitude to my colleague Wayne Marshall Jones for his coaching, consultation, editing, proofreading, and book/cover design. His steadfast dedication and attention to detail are invaluable. His knowledge and skill base have been instrumental in bringing forth the Living in Alignment body of work.

I offer gratitude to my beloved cat Bodhi, who has been the mascot for this project. His love and affection have helped sustain me for the duration of this endeavor.

I offer gratitude to my late mother Jeannine for offering her abiding love, support, and encouragement to live authentically and for fostering my spirituality.

To all of you I express my heartfelt appreciation.

Darcy S. Clarke MA LPCC CADC-II CTPC